Computing for the Older Generation

Jim Gatenby

BERNARD BABANI (publishing) LTD
The Grampians
Shepherds Bush Road
London W6 7NF
England

www.babanibooks.com

Please Note

Although every care has been taken with the production of this book to ensure that any projects, designs, modifications and/or programs, etc., contained herewith, operate in a correct and safe manner and also that any components specified are normally available in Great Britain, the Publishers and Author do not accept responsibility in any way for the failure (including fault in design) of any project, design, modification or program to work correctly or to cause damage to any equipment that it may be connected to or used in conjunction with, or in respect of any other damage or injury that may be so caused, nor do the Publishers accept responsibility in any way for the failure to obtain specified components.

Notice is also given that if equipment that is still under warranty is modified in any way or used or connected with home-built equipment then that warranty may be void.

First published - February 2003
Reprinted - May 2003
Reprinted - August 2003
Reprinted - October 2003
Reprinted - December 2003
Reprinted - January 2004
Reprinted - February 2004
Reprinted - March 2004
Reprinted - April 2004
Reprinted - June 2004
Reprinted - July 2004
Reprinted - September 2004
Reprinted - October 2004
Reprinted - November 2004
Reprinted - December 2004
Reprinted - February 2005 (twice)
Reprinted - March 2005

British Library Cataloguing in Publication Data

A catalogue record for this book is available from the British Library

ISBN 0 85934 601 3

Cover Design by Gregor Arthur

Printed and bound in Great Britain by Cox & Wyman Ltd, Reading, Berks

Computing for the
Older Generation

Other Books of Interest

About this Book

For various reasons, many older people feel they have missed out on the computing revolution of the last few decades. This book attempts to show, in plain English, that older people have much to gain by owning and using a computer. Computer jargon is avoided wherever possible.

The first chapter describes the way computers evolved over recent years and outlines many of the ways a computer can enrich later life. These include keeping in touch with friends and family by e-mail, organising records for a hobby and starting a new career or business. The next few chapters describe the main parts of a computer system with advice on buying and upgrading, including a list of questions for potential suppliers. Advice is given on setting up a computer in the home, with consideration for health and safety issues. The latest Microsoft Windows XP system installed on many computers is described, including built-in help for users with impaired mobility, hearing and eyesight.

Later chapters cover the main software applications, word processing, spreadsheets, desktop publishing and database and practice exercises and skills checklists are included. The Internet is described towards the end of the book, including searching for information on virtually any subject, tracing of family trees and e-mailing friends and family around the world, with photographs as attachments. The final chapter shows how your computer can be used as a competent music and video centre.

As a member of the over 50's club myself, I have considerable experience of teaching people of all ages. Since retiring from teaching I have used my own computer, working from home, to build a second career as an author.

About the Author

Jim Gatenby trained as a Chartered Mechanical Engineer and initially worked at Rolls-Royce Ltd using computers in the analysis of performance. He obtained a Master of Philosophy degree in Mathematical Education by research at Loughborough University of Technology and taught mathematics and computing to 'A' Level for many years. His most recent posts included Head of Computer Studies and Information Technology Coordinator. During this time he has written many books in the fields of educational computing and Microsoft Windows.

The author has considerable experience of teaching students of all ages and abilities, in school and in adult education. For several years he successfully taught the well-established CLAIT course and also GCSE Computing and Information Technology.

Contents

1

2

3

7

Help for Users with Special Needs   101

8

Introducing Microsoft Works   111

9

Word Processing   127

10

Editing a Document   145

11

Desktop Publishing   167

15

Using the Internet   265

16

The Windows Media Player   295

Index   305

Computers in Context

Introduction

Older people (including myself) have witnessed the phenomenal growth in the use of computers in the last 40 years or so. However, many of us were not directly involved in this revolution. Some older people feel they have missed out on the benefits of the new technology and others may feel it's too late to catch up.

This chapter describes the evolution of computers in the second half of the 20th century and attempts to explain why some older people may have doubts about their ability to benefit from using computers. This chapter is also intended to show that it's never too late to learn about computers and that older people have nothing to fear and much to gain from using the new technology.

Those of us born more than 50 years ago left school having used nothing more complex than log tables and perhaps early calculating machines. My first experience of computers was in industry in the early 1960s, when massive machines occupying whole rooms were used mainly for calculating work.

These early machines were used mainly by specialists such as mathematicians, scientists and engineers. Special new languages had to be learned to give instructions to the machines. Sets of instructions for a particular task were known as *programs* and this gave rise to the new profession of *computer programmer*.

In these early years the use of computers was confined within the separate computing departments of large organizations, employing specialist staff. Advances in computing tended to bypass the general public; for example, secretaries and typists were still using manual and electric typewriters. Many people therefore saw the use of computers as an activity only for the technical specialist.

The Arrival of the Microcomputer

This situation started to change in the late 1970's with the arrival of the desktop microcomputer, which was to make computing available to a wider audience. Schools and home users could now afford to buy a small computer. These included the Sinclair ZX81 introduced in 1981. In those days it was still necessary to learn a special programming language and to write complex instructions in order to make the computer do anything.

Courses sprang up around the country, teaching people how to program the new machines. Most of the tasks still involved calculating work. Indeed, when computers were first introduced in school, they were usually part of the mathematics department. So anyone who didn't like maths was hardly likely to embrace computers with great enthusiasm.

The Development of Software

 Magnetic tapes and discs were developed, allowing programs to be saved, instead of being typed in using a keyboard. Soon a new industry evolved, selling ready-made programs stored on disc, collectively known as *software*.

This software was not just for calculating work; for example, the *word processor* was one of the first applications of microcomputers, later to revolutionize the office with many advantages over the ordinary typewriter.

However, it was still necessary to use the keyboard to type in *commands* to carry out tasks such as printing a letter on paper or saving the text onto a magnetic disc. Some of these commands were quite complex and were very off-putting to the ordinary user. The slightest mistake in the spelling or punctuation would cause a command to fail. Many people were too busy with their everyday work to find the time needed to learn the new skills.

Other people embraced the microcomputer with great enthusiasm. Some of these enthusiasts, nowadays referred to with the derogatory title of "nerds" or "anoraks", took great pride in the specialist computing knowledge they quickly acquired, with a zeal sometimes bordering on addiction.

Unfortunately, some of these enthusiasts would use their new-found specialist knowledge to show off. Often their amateurish attempts at "training" other colleagues only had the effect of making quite normal and competent people feel stupid and apathetic about working with computers.

In the early days, computers were often introduced into companies without proper staff training, so that employees became frustrated and antagonistic towards the machines. Expensive new equipment was not always fully utilized and sometimes stood idle or locked away in cupboards.

Computers Become Easier to Use

The software manufacturers, aware that computers were still regarded as difficult to use by the general public, began to look for ways to make the machines more "user friendly". Instead of typing in complex instructions in a "foreign" language, the user was presented with a menu, or list of choices on the screen. To choose a task, such as printing a letter on paper, it was simply a case of selecting the task using various keys on the keyboard.

The Mouse

The next milestone in making computers easy to use was the arrival of the *mouse*. This is a small hand-held device with either two or three buttons. The mouse is usually attached to the computer by a cable. Moving the mouse about  the desk causes a small pointer to move about the screen. Now to select a task or object on the screen, the pointer is moved over the task and a button (usually the left-hand button) is pressed on the mouse.

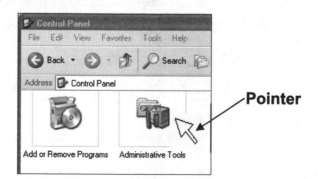

So the computer could now be controlled simply by moving the mouse pointer about the screen and "clicking" a button when the pointer is over the required task. The mouse can also be used for freehand drawing and painting on the screen. In this new system, many of the common operations were represented by small pictures or *icons*. For example, to print a letter you would use the mouse to point

 and click at a printer icon on the screen. Now there was no longer any need to remember complex commands to be typed in at the keyboard.

Introducing Windows

With this new mouse controlled system, various parts of the screen were divided up into rectangular boxes known as *windows*. A screen may contain several windows at a time. For example, a window for a word processing document such as a letter might appear alongside another window for a painting program. The user can work on either document by using the mouse to switch to the appropriate window.

The screen below shows a painting program and a word processing document each running in their own window.

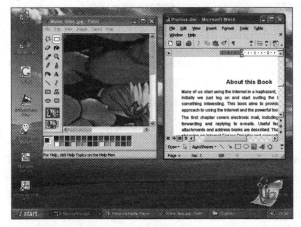

Also shown on the previous screenshot are various icons or small pictures representing different tasks. Any of these tasks can be started using the mouse and its pointer. For example, clicking the icon shown on the left would start up Google, a very popular *search engine*. This is a program designed to help you find information on the Internet.

Menus and Icons

Most modern programs work in a similar way. Shown below is part of the screen for one of the world's most popular programs, Microsoft Word. This is used for producing letters, reports and books (such as this one).

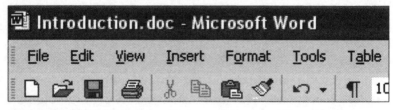

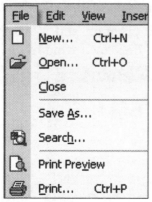

Shown above is part of the *menu bar* which is displayed across the top of the Microsoft Word screen, above the work area where you type your letters, etc. When you click any of the words on the menu bar such as **File** or **Edit**, a menu drops down in its own window, as shown on the left. For example, to start typing on a new blank page you would click the word **New...** as shown on the left. For those who prefer to use the keyboard, a new document can also be started by pressing the key marked **Ctrl** together with the **N** key.

As can be seen, some commands can also be launched using an icon, such as the command to start a new document in a word processor, as shown on the right. Icons are displayed along the bottom of the menu bar as shown on the previous page and in more detail below.

You can see the purpose of each icon by allowing the on-screen cursor to dwell over the icon. This causes a short explanation to appear below the icon, as shown on the right.

You will find the same icons are used in many different programs. You might, for example, start off using a word processor for your correspondence then move on to a spreadsheet program for your household accounts or a database for your records and catalogues. When you have learned to use one program you will find it easy to learn others - they all work in a similar fashion.

This new method of working involves **Windows**, **Icons**, a **Mouse** and a **Pointer** and is known as a "WIMP" system. As its purpose to control or operate the computer, it's known as an *operating system*. The WIMP system was pioneered by the Xerox Company and first made popular on Apple computers such as the Macintosh, which acquired many devotees because it was so easy to use.

Microsoft Windows

Most of the microcomputers in the world now use software made by the dominant Microsoft Company. In 1990 Microsoft brought out its own WIMP operating system, known as Microsoft Windows. The intervening years have seen several different versions of Microsoft Windows including Windows 3.1, Windows 95, Windows 98, Windows NT, Windows Me and currently Windows XP.

Microsoft Windows (or simply "Windows") is discussed in more detail later in this book. The screenshot below shows the **start** menu for Windows XP, the latest version of Microsoft Windows.

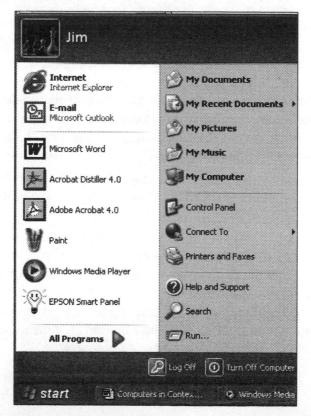

Computer Whiz Kids and Older Users

There's no doubt that many older people are anxious about using computers, perhaps feeling they are too difficult to learn, especially when so many young children appear to be computer "whiz kids". As an experienced teacher of computing to students of all ages from 11 to 80 years I know that older people can make very good use of computers either in their own business or employment or to enhance their hobbies and daily life in retirement.

In recent years it has been compulsory for children to use computers, so that on leaving school students should be able to cope with the widespread use of computers in most areas of employment. In addition, many children have computers and video games in their bedrooms, so from an early age they are familiar and comfortable with computing equipment such as keyboards and mice. On the negative side, excessive use of electronic games (rather than games involving physical exercise) has been blamed for an increase in obesity amongst children in recent years.

However, there is no doubt that younger people have generally grown up with greater confidence in the use of computers than many of the older generation. On the other hand, while many children *appear* to be computing geniuses simply because of their prowess at playing games, older people have the experience to use computers sensibly to do useful and interesting work. Older people often have the time to learn new skills and also the patience to persevere with problems.

As shown in the following list, there are many applications of computers which can be both interesting and beneficial to older people.

Making Good Use of a Computer

Modern computers are extremely versatile. Here are a few sample applications, though the list is far from exhaustive. Many of these examples are described in more detail later in this book or in the companion text "The Internet for the Older Generation", reference BP600, from Bernard Babani (publishing) Ltd.

- Keeping in touch with relatives and friends using letters and e-mails. Creating publications such as reports, magazines, posters and newsletters.

- Keeping track of your household expenses.

- Cataloguing records for a small business or a hobby such as plants, recipes or a music collection.

- Storing digital photographs on your computer and editing and enhancing them to make quality prints.

- Using the Internet to find accurate and up-to-date information on any subject including your ancestry and family tree, common illnesses and financial planning.

- Using the Internet for on-line shopping. For example, ordering books from Amazon, finding out about holiday destinations and booking accommodation.

- Carrying out supermarket shopping on-line. This is quick and easy and saves the undoubted stress and hard work of traditional supermarket shopping.

- Creating on your computer, a library of your music, which can be played in the background while you work.

- Using a home computer to run a small business or start a second career. Since retiring from teaching I have produced several books at home, typeset and ready for printing, avoiding the hassle of commuting.

Some Reassuring Facts About Computers

If, after reading this chapter, you are still anxious about using computers for the first time, here are a few facts which may help to allay some common fears:

Modern computers are easy to use

Most modern computer programs are operated by selecting from menus and small icons (pictures) on the screen, using a mouse and on-screen pointer. The general method is easy to learn and this same method can then be used for all sorts of different tasks. Modern computers are therefore extremely easy for *anyone* to use.

You don't need to be good at maths or electronics to use a computer

Most computing activities do not involve maths or any sort of technical work - typical uses include writing letters, sending messages by e-mail or designing posters and leaflets. You don't need any special training to make good use of computers, although you may benefit from a confidence-building course or short courses tailored to help with particular tasks.

Modern computers can produce excellent results

Advances in software such as word processors and desktop publishing and also cheap inkjet and laser printers mean that anyone can produce professional looking publications.

Older people have significant advantages

Many older people have the time to learn new skills at their own pace and to attend day-time courses. They usually have a wealth of experience enabling them to plan and organize their work and set realistic targets.

You can't easily lose all of your work

With sensible precautions (discussed later in this book) you can easily make regular "backup" copies of important work to protect yourself against possible disaster.

You can't easily damage the computer itself

In normal use it is most unlikely that the computer or your work can be damaged by making a mistake while typing at the keyboard. Computer "viruses" (small programs designed by computing "vandals" to damage data files) can be spread through e-mails sent via the telephone lines. However, you can guard against these by installing up-to-date *anti-virus software* (discussed later in this book). Viruses only damage the data stored on your computer, they don't damage the physical components, known as *hardware*. In fact, the hardware is most unlikely to be damaged under any circumstances, except by careless handling or the spilling of drinks (and, of course, major disasters such as fire, floods or theft).

Modern computers are reliable

If handled with care, modern computers are generally robust and reliable. Obviously constant moving about is likely to cause problems. Making acquaintance with a reliable, local computer repair specialist is always a good idea should you be unlucky and have a major fault.

Help and support is readily available

Most software has built-in help and further support is available by telephoning or e-mailing the manufacturers. At a local level, there are usually beginners' courses either free or for a modest fee. The popular CLAIT courses offered at local colleges lead to qualifications in basic software skills and are widely recognized by employers.

2

The Main Parts of a Computer System

Introduction

This chapter discusses the main parts which make up a computer system. Although there are variations in the price and performance of computer systems, they all contain the same set of basic components. A typical system is shown below.

The main parts of this basic system shown above are:

- The *tower* or *base unit* shown on the left.
- The *keyboard* with the *mouse* to the right.
- The *monitor* or *VDU* (Visual Display Unit).
- The *printer*, in this case a small laser printer.

The *base unit* is at the heart of the system. Nowadays the base unit is often in the form of a *tower*, which can stand upright on the floor, thereby saving desk space. This allows more space for other components, such as a scanner and speakers, to be placed on the desk, as shown below.

Desktop base units consist of flat boxes designed to sit on the desk with the monitor (or screen) on top.

The base unit contains the essential components of the computer, such as the *processor*, the *memory*, the *motherboard*, the *hard disc drive*, the *CD drive* and the *floppy disc drive*. These parts, normally hidden from view under the metal case of the base unit, are described in the next chapter, **Inside the Computer**. The components in the base unit are connected to the main circuit board of the computer, known as the *motherboard*. Other components which make up the computer system, such as the mouse, keyboard, monitor and printer, sit outside of the base unit and are known as *peripheral* units.

The peripheral units connect to the motherboard via cables plugged into sockets on the back of the base unit. These sockets are known as *ports*.

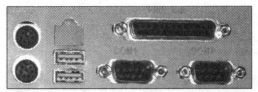

The Keyboard

Keyboards have been around since the first typewriters but they have not yet been replaced, to any great extent, by modern inventions such as voice recognition systems.

Most keyboards still follow the QWERTY convention, which refers to the order of the first six letter keys.

Some Important Keys

Capital letters are obtained by simultaneously holding the

Shift key, shown left and below, marked with an upward pointing arrow. Or you can switch the **Caps Lock** key on and off as required.

Where there are two characters on a key, the upper character is obtained by holding down the **Shift** key while the required key is pressed.

The screenshot below shows another set of important keys on the right of the keyboard.

The cluster of numeric keys on the right above is the *numeric key pad*. This is often used when a large amount of numeric data is to be entered continuously.

The four keys marked with arrows are the *cursor control keys*. These can be used to move the cursor about the screen or to step through the options on a menu. Along the top of the keyboard are the *function keys*, marked **F1** to **F12**. These can be programmed to carry out various functions. For example, **F1** is often programmed to provide help within a piece of software.

The **Backspace** key is used to delete text to the left of the current cursor position. The **Delete** key removes text to the right of the current cursor position.

Also shown are duplicates of the **Shift** and **Ctrl** keys, which are also present on the left of the keyboard.

The **Enter** key shown left and on the numeric keypad on the previous page, is used to start a new line when typing. It is also known as the **Return** key, after the term Carriage Return on ordinary typewriters.

The **Insert** key shown left allows you to switch between **Insert** and **Overtype** mode. In **Insert** mode, any letters you type in the middle of a sentence push out the existing letters. In **Overtype** mode the existing letters disappear as you type over them.

The **Home** key moves the cursor to the beginning of a *line of text*. The **End** key moves the cursor to the end of a *line*.

Ctrl+Home and **Ctrl+End** move the cursor to the beginning and end of a *document*.

Page Up and **Page Down** enable you to scroll through a document approximately one *screen* at a time.

Ctrl+Page Up and **Ctrl+Page down** enable you to scroll through a document a *page* at a time.

At the bottom of the keyboard, the long key (shown below) is the **Space Bar**, used to insert spaces between words.

Also shown above and below is the **Windows** key, which brings up the Microsoft Windows **start** menu.

If you don't possess typing skills you may wish to practice with one of the many typing tutor programs available such as Mavis Beacon Teaches Typing. If you learn to type properly, apart from saving time, this will allow you to concentrate on the screen and the content of your work, rather than constantly looking for keys on the keyboard.

Keyboard Shortcuts

Many people are happy to operate the computer using a mouse, by pointing and clicking over screen icons and menus. However, others, particularly trained typists, prefer to use the keyboard for everything.

As an alternative to using the mouse, many operations can be carried out using special combinations of key presses, known as *keyboard shortcuts*. For example, to turn bold text *on* you would press the key marked **Ctrl** together with the key for the letter **B**. To turn bold text *off* you would again press **Ctrl+B**.

In general, if an effect is turned on by a keyboard shortcut, it is turned off by the same method. Keyboard shortcuts are discussed again in the chapter on word processing.

Microsoft Keyboards

Special Microsoft Windows keyboards are available which contain, amongst other things, small round buttons for connecting directly to the Internet and searching for particular Web pages. Special buttons also give direct access to Windows features such as a **Calculator** and **My Computer**, which displays information about your discs and files.

An *on-screen keyboard* is provided in Windows XP to help anyone with restricted movement. The virtual keyboard is displayed on the screen as shown below. The mouse is then used to select the required key on the screen. Clicking a letter or number causes that character to appear in the document on the screen at the current cursor position.

The Mouse

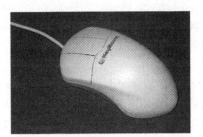

As discussed in the previous chapter, the mouse is used to:

- Select icons from a menu on the screen.
- Start programs from a screen icon.
- Open a "folder" containing documents.
- Draw or paint freehand.

Shown below is the Windows **start** menu. Any of the programs or features can be launched by clicking the left mouse button over the appropriate name or icon.

The mouse can also be used to "drag and drop" objects on the screen. As discussed later, in the section on Microsoft Windows, files of documents are stored in folders which can be displayed on the screen.

A document can be moved between folders by dragging and dropping. This involves moving the mouse pointer over an object then *keeping the left mouse button held down* while the object is dragged to its new position. Then the left mouse button is released.

For example, the screenshot below shows 3 folders and one document called **Draft Contents.doc**. The document could be moved and stored in any of the folders by dragging and dropping as described above.

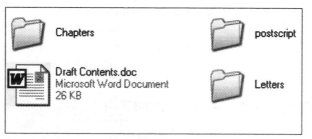

Managing documents and folders in this way is described in more detail later in this book.

Mice normally have two or three buttons. Even with a three button mouse, most programs only use the left and right buttons. The left-hand button is used to select objects on the screen. Some operations require a single click while others need a "double click" - two clicks of the left button in rapid succession.

In some programs, the right-hand mouse button can be used to cancel or undo the most recent operation.

The right button can also be used to display *pop-up menus* relevant to the current cursor position. These menus appear wherever you click on the screen, unlike *drop-down menus* which appear under the menu bar at the top of the screen. For example, pressing the right mouse button over the text in a word processing document would bring up the following menu in Microsoft Word.

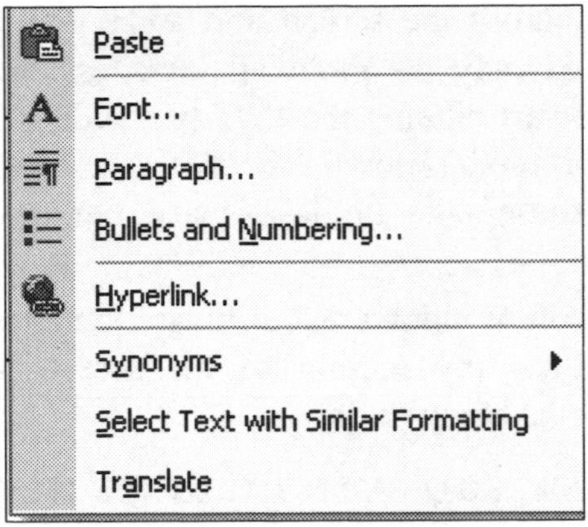

The settings of the mouse can be adjusted in Microsoft Windows. For example, you can switch the functions of the left and right buttons or alter the appearance of the on-screen pointer, as shown on the right.

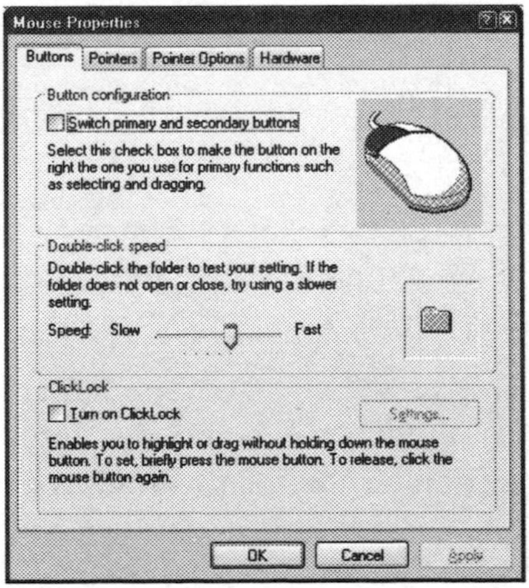

The Monitor

The choice of monitor (or screen) depends on how much you want to spend. If you intend to do a lot of exacting work such as DeskTop Publishing or Graphics, or if you have impaired vision, you may be wise to invest in a large screen size. 15inch, 17inch and 19inch monitors are common today. These measurements are measured diagonally across the screen and are nominal. The actual viewing area may be about an inch less, because of the plastic case surrounding the *CRT* (Cathode Ray Tube). Flat screen monitors (known as *TFT* monitors) are now available; these take up less space but are much more expensive.

The Microsoft Windows XP software includes a Magnifier which enables any section of the screen to be viewed enlarged, in its own window.

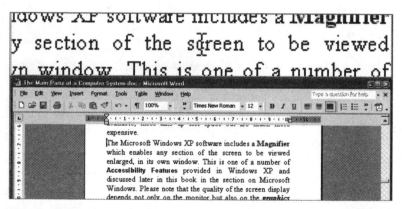

This is one of a number of **Accessibility Features** provided in Windows XP and discussed later in this book in the section on Microsoft Windows.

Please note that the quality of the screen display depends not only on the monitor but also on the *graphics card,* an expansion card plugged into the computer's motherboard. Any computer you buy will contain a graphics card as standard. Some people choose to replace the standard graphics card with a higher performance model. This is usually to improve the screen display of graphics on computer games and simulations, for example.

As discussed later in this book, Microsoft Windows allows you to adjust the colours used to display the various menus and windows. You can also adjust the screen *resolution.* The resolution is the number of small squares (known as *pixels* or *picture elements*) used to map out the screen. Typical screen resolutions are 800x600 and 1024x768, as shown below.

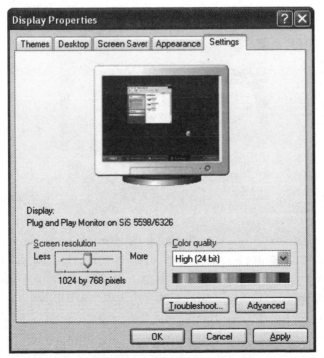

The Printer

A reliable printer is an essential part of your computer system - you can't do all of your communication by e-mail or posting on Web sites. A printer is needed to produce paper copies of letters, reports, accounts, publications, magazines, photographs, e-mails and Web pages.

Nowadays there are two popular types of printer used in the home and small business. These are the *laser printer* and the *inkjet*. You need to consider the type of work you will be doing in order to choose a suitable printer.

The Inkjet Printer

Inkjet printers are good all-rounders and can be bought for as little as £50, although models costing several hundred pounds are also available.

You must also consider the cost of the ink cartridges (both black and colour) which can cost from £10-£20 or more. Inkjet printers can produce high quality colour photographs, though the cost of the cartridges and the special glossy paper makes this quite an expensive activity.

The Laser Printer

Laser printers are popular in business. They are fast, produce high quality printout and tend to be quieter than inkjets. Most laser printers are *mono* (i.e. they print only in black and white.) Perfectly good mono laser printers can be bought for less than £200, while colour laser printers are still very expensive (from about £1000 upwards). I have been using an HP LaserJet printer as shown below. This cost about £250 nearly 6 years and is still going strong.

Laser printers use a black powder called *toner* and the toner cartridge must be replaced periodically. A new laser toner cartridge may typically cost around £50, but this may be capable of printing several thousand sheets of A4 paper.

Dot-matrix printers used to be popular as they are quite fast and can print on continuous rolls of paper. The dot-matrix is not suitable for publications where quality is important. The dot-matrix printer has lost out to the higher quality of the laser printer and the colour and quality of the inkjet.

The Scanner

The scanner is an optional extra rather than an essential part of a computer system. A common type is the A4 flatbed scanner, a flat box roughly the size of  a large folder, as shown. Scanners cost from about £50 upwards.

An image of a piece of paper containing text and/or graphics can be copied and inserted into a document on the screen. Alternatively the scanned image can be saved on your hard disc or sent to a range of destinations such as e-mail or the Web. As shown from the following menu (for an Epson scanner), the scanner can also copy a document straight to your printer, acting like a photocopier. The scanner is considerably slower than a photocopier and suitable for only a few copies. The scanner is also useful for copying old photographs into a program such as Paint Shop Pro, where they can be edited and improved before printing.

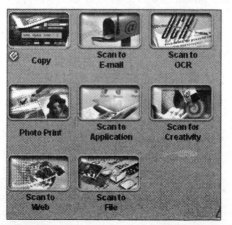

The Modem

The modem is a small set of microchips used to connect a computer to the Internet via the telephone lines. *External modems* are contained in their own box and sit outside of

the computer on the desk. A cable connects the modem to the back of the computer and another cable plugs into the standard telephone line. The external modem has an array of indicator lights which report on the current activities – such as whether the modem is switched on, or if it is sending or receiving data, fax or voice mail, etc. The external modem is portable - it can easily be unplugged and transferred to another computer. The external modem requires an extra power point and cables, unlike the internal modem.

The *Internal Modem* consists of a small circuit board containing a set of chips. This plugs inside of the case of

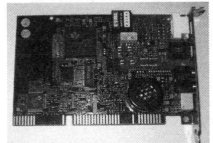

the computer, out of sight. The internal modem obviously saves desk space and is more secure from damage or possible theft. The internal version takes its power off the computer itself.

The modem is still the most popular method of connecting to the Internet, certainly for the home user. There are faster "broadband" alternatives such as cable modems and ADSL but currently these are relatively expensive and are not yet available to users in all areas of Britain.

Most modems are currently classed as "56K", a figure relating to the speed with which they can receive data (text, pictures, etc.,) from the Internet. "K" in the context of modems stands for *kilobits* per second, a measure of the speed of the modem when sending and receiving data. (A keyboard character is represented by 8 bits, a kilobit being approximately 1000 bits). The speed with which you can *receive* data (56K) is greater than the speed you can *send* data to other computers (often only about 33K).

Whereas the conventional 56K modem has a nominal data transmission rate of 56 kilobits per second, some cable modems can exceed a rate of one *megabit* (approximately one million bits) per second. Broadband connections are generally claimed to be at least 10 times faster than traditional modems. Power hungry applications such as the "streaming" (i.e. broadcasting) and downloading of moving video from the Internet require this extra speed. In the long-term therefore, the traditional "analogue" modem is likely to be superseded by the more powerful broadband systems. However, until recently the take-up of broadband technology in Britain has been slow and the modem is expected to be in widespread use for several years to come.

With the latest Internet connections, communications can involve much more than e-mail and surfing the Web. *Video conferencing* has been around for some years in business. Two computers connected across the Internet can share live voice and moving video links. So friends and families across the world can see moving pictures of each other while talking.

The Digital Camera

This is one of the latest developments in computing. Cheap digital cameras can be bought for as little as £40, while better quality ones may cost several hundred pounds. Some new computer systems currently on offer include a free digital camera. The digital camera doesn't use film, but instead has a memory. The images are stored in the memory until you "download" them to your computer. This is done by connecting the camera to the computer using a special cable, include in the camera package. Software provided with the camera makes this an extremely simple task. Another cable allows you to connect your camera to a television set and view the photos on the TV screen.

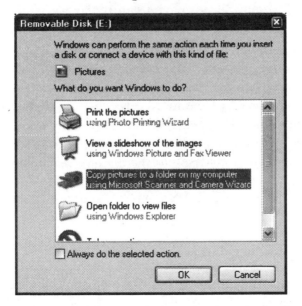

Once in your computer, the images can be edited in a program such as Paint Shop Pro 7 before being printed on special glossy photographic paper.

You will also be supplied with some basic AA batteries to get you started but you will need to replace these with some rechargeable ones (Nickel-Cadmium or Nickel-Metal Hydride). A set of these together with a charger costs about £15.

The memory in a digital camera often consists of a plug-in module such as the *SmartMedia* card, as used on Olympus cameras, for example. The memory itself is mounted on a thin plastic material about the size of a large postage stamp. The card is a push fit in the body of the camera. An 8 MB card is often supplied as standard with a new camera. This has the capacity to store up to 47 images, before they have to be downloaded to the computer. If this memory is not enough for your purposes you can replace it with a bigger memory card. For example, a 16 MB would currently cost about £11.

Some digital cameras are equipped with flash and a zoom lens. Others have a small preview screen allowing you to view the set of images stored in the memory and delete any you don't want. Some digital cameras also allow you to record a few minutes of video. This can be viewed in the small monitor on the back of the camera or on a television screen.

Next

The next chapter, Inside the Computer, describes the main components inside the case of the base unit. These are at the heart of the computer and determine how your computer will perform. It's worth familiarizing yourself with them, if only so that you are not bamboozled by the sales staff when you are choosing your first computer.

Inside the Computer

Introduction

The base unit is the metal box containing the essential parts of the computer. The base unit is really the computer itself. It could start up and run without the peripheral units like the keyboard, mouse and printer, although you wouldn't be able to do much with it. The peripheral units are for *inputting* data, etc., into the computer and for displaying or printing information *output* from the computer. In the example shown on the right, the base unit is in the form of a tower, usually situated on the  floor. Desktop base units are also available as flat boxes on which the monitor can be placed.

At the top of the base unit shown above is the CD drive, with space underneath for additional drives such as a DVD drive (after first removing the plastic blanking strip). The smallest slot at the bottom is the floppy disc drive. On the right is the main power switch for the computer. There is also a light which flashes on and off to indicate hard disc activity and a light to show if the computer is switched on.

The Processor

This is the "brains" of the computer and carries out all of the instructions sent into the processor by the program you are using. Well known brands are the Intel Pentium and the AMD Athlon. The speed at which the processor works determines the performance of the computer. Currently new computers are being advertised offering processor speeds of around 2GHz. This is a measure of how many thousands of millions of instructions per second the processor can carry out.

Machines with faster processors are available at a greater price. As a general rule, if you are intending to use your computer for tasks such as word processing, publishing documents, keeping accounts and records, sending and receiving e-mails and searching the Internet, then a basic processor of perhaps 1 or 2GHz will be quite good enough.

It's certainly not necessary for the general user to keep up with all the latest offerings from the processor manufacturers. For example, I am currently using a machine with a 1GHz processor and this is quite satisfactory for the sort of use described above.

If you later find that you need a more powerful processor, it may be possible to "upgrade" your existing computer. Check before buying a new system whether the processor can be upgraded at a later date. It may simply be a case of unplugging the old processor and replacing it with the new one. This is much cheaper than buying a new computer.

The Memory

The memory (also known as RAM or Random Access Memory) is a set of microchips which act as a store for the data or information typed in at the keyboard. The memory also holds the programs that you are currently using. The memory is only a *temporary store*. Like the processor, the size of the memory can have a major effect on the performance of the computer. Modern programs, with all of their graphics, windows and icons, demand massive amounts of memory. Photographs are also very hungry for memory.

If your computer is short of memory, programs will run very slowly. Therefore it's best to buy a computer with as much memory as possible. Currently machines are being sold with 256 or 512MB of memory. If buying a new machine, aim for at least 256MB to start off with. Memory is usually relatively cheap, although prices do fluctuate. It's a 10 minute job to plug extra memory into the computer at a later date. Expect to pay about £30 for the extra memory or RAM chips, also known as SIMMs.

Any data (text, etc.) stored in the memory during a computing session is lost as soon as the computer is switched off. Any data you wish to keep must be saved on a magnetic storage medium such as your hard disc drive, discussed shortly.

The Hard Disc Drive

The hard disc drive is a sealed unit built inside of the computer. You won't ever see your hard disc drive unless you remove the computer's metal casing. The magnetic disc surfaces on which programs and data are recorded are an integral part of the drive unit, which also contains the heads used for reading and writing data.

The hard disc is usually designated as the **C:** drive, and consists of a set of metal discs, coated in a magnetic material and rotating about a central spindle. The hard disc unit is housed in a metal case and is sealed to prevent particles of dust from entering and damaging the disc surfaces, which are machined to very fine tolerances.

In normal use the hard disc rotates at several thousand revolutions per minute. This makes it very fast at saving and retrieving data. However, the computer should not be moved or knocked while the computer is running as this might cause the hard disc to "crash".

If the moving head which "reads" the data from the disc touches one of the disc surfaces (resulting in a "head crash"), the disc surface will be scratched and some, if not all, of the data may be lost.

The amount of data which can be stored on a hard disc is normally measured in *megabytes* (*MB*) or *gigabytes* (*GB*). A megabyte is roughly a million keyboard characters and a gigabyte is roughly 1000 megabytes. A recent book similar to this one, consisting of text and screenshots (but without photographs), occupied about 20MB. This could easily be saved on a modern hard disc consisting of 80GB or roughly 80,000MB. It could also be backed up onto a CD with a typical capacity of 700MB.

The Contents of the Hard Disc Drive

The hard disc inside of the computer is like the filing cabinet in a traditional office. Permanently saved on the magnetic surfaces of the hard disc are the programs and data essential for the running of the computer.

When you switch the computer off, the contents of the hard disc remain in place (barring disasters). The hard disc normally contains:

- The *systems software* such as the Windows operating system needed to start and run the computer.

- The *applications software* (programs) such as your word processor, database, desktop publishing (DTP) and Internet browser.

- The work you have produced and saved as *files* - such as the word processing documents, spreadsheets, graphics files, music, photographs and Web pages captured from the Internet.

The hard disc is generally a robust component which can perform reliably for many thousands of hours over several years. However, due to possible accidents and disasters such as fire and floods, it is possible for individuals and companies to "lose" the entire contents of a hard disc.

In some cases the files of data may still exist on the disc after a disaster, but the ordinary user can't retrieve them by normal methods. (There are companies specialising in the recovery of data from damaged hard discs but this can be an expensive process).

As discussed later in this book, important work should always be "backed up", i.e. a duplicate copy made on a separate disc or CD.

The Floppy Disc

The name floppy disc originated with the earlier 5.25 inch disc, which really was "floppy". Some people mistakenly think that the 3.5 inch "floppy" disc used today, because of its rigid plastic case, is actually a "hard" disc. In fact,  the magnetic disc material (known as the "cookie") inside the plastic case of the 3.5 inch disc is really quite flexible and "floppy". The 3.5 inch disc or "diskette" is portable and very easily inserted into or removed from the floppy disc drive. In the past, most new software packages were supplied on one or more floppy discs. Now, with the vastly increased size of new software packages, this role has been taken over by the CD-ROM. Transferring files from a single CD is much faster and less prone to errors than from a large number of 3.5 inch diskettes.

However, the 3.5 inch disc is still a very cheap and convenient way of transferring a few files or a small piece of software from one computer to another. For example, if you want to save a document then take it home and carry on working on it. It's also a quick way to make a backup copy of important files for security purposes, provided they can fit on the floppy disc, with its limited capacity of 1.44MB. (Compare this with the CD, which has a typical capacity of 700MB.) The floppy disc drive is usually called the **A:** drive.

Floppy Discs and Viruses

Floppy discs can be a source of viruses. Always check discs you have received from elsewhere, with an up-to-date anti-virus program as described later in this book.

Expansion Cards

Sitting inside of the case of you computer are a number of small circuit boards, known as expansion cards. These plug into the motherboard of the computer and often have a cable connector at back of the main computer base unit.

Some expansion cards are essential and are already present in a new computer. These include the *graphics card* and usually a *sound card*. Other cards may be added later to add extra functions to the computer, (hence the term "expansion card"). These might include an *internal modem* which is supplied on an expansion card, as shown below.

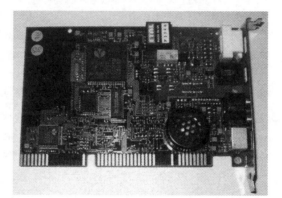

The CD Drive and CD Media

Although CDs have been around for a long time, only in the last few years has it been possible, at an affordable price, to write and rewrite your own CDs. Originally, when most CD drives were "read only", you might buy a CD containing a new piece of software. This had to be copied onto your computer's hard disc. Then you could use the software whenever you wanted to, without putting the CD in the drive. The CD is still the main medium for supplying new software.

The CD is also used for providing vast quantities of information which you can search, such as an encyclopedia or a set of back copies of a magazine.

Nowadays the CD is more versatile. The main breakthrough is that the user can now "write" to the CD, so that you can make copies of your work. This is a cheap and convenient form of storage either as a backup or for sending work to another person. For example, when this book is finished it will be copied onto a CD and posted to the printers. The CD has a storage capacity equivalent to *several hundred* floppy discs.

Microsoft Windows XP includes its own software for "burning" or copying files onto a CD. If your computer has an earlier version of Microsoft Windows, you can buy CD burning software separately, such as Nero from Ahead Software and Easy CD Creator from Roxio.

CD Media

There are two main types of writeable CD media:

The **CD-R** disc can be written to only once, after which it can only be used for reading operations. CD-R discs currently cost around 50p or less.

The **CD-RW** disc can be used repeatedly for writing and rewriting. First it must be formatted to prepare it for the recording process, known as "Packet Writing".

This allows the CD-RW disc to be used like a floppy or hard disc, with drag and drop copying operations, etc. CD-RW discs are currently priced at around £1 each. If you buy a CD-RW drive, it can be used to read normal data and audio CD-ROMs, to "burn" CD-R discs in a once only operation, and to format, write and rewrite CD-RWs.

Advertisements for CD-RW drives normally state performance in terms of writing, rewriting and reading speeds. For example, 44/24/44 means:

> Writes at 44 speed (6600KB/s)
>
> Rewrites at 24 speed (3600KB/s)
>
> Reads at 44 speed (6600KB/s)

Some CD drives can also play the newer DVD discs. These are very high capacity discs capable of storing a full-length movie. Some new computers are fitted with separate CD and DVD drives. The DVD drive is much more expensive than the CD drive.

Later versions of Microsoft Windows, such as Windows Me and Windows XP, contain a program called the Windows Media Player. Amongst other things, this software allows you to copy music from an audio CD onto your hard disc. Then you can organize your favourite records into separate *playlists*. These can be played in the background (without using the CD) while you are working on the computer.

The CD drive is often designated as the **D:** drive and sometimes the **E:** drive. (If **D:** has already been allocated to some other device, such as a second hard disc drive.)

CDs and Multi-media

Small speakers which plug into the back of your computer can be bought costing anything from about £10 upwards. These help to turn a computer into a complete multi-media centre. Apart from playing music, you can also use software with sound effects or a voice commentary. For example, the Microsoft Flight Simulator, which includes impressive graphics, video clips and sound is so realistic that it's used by trainee pilots for additional practice.

Planning for the Future - Upgradeability

As previously stated, computers rapidly become obsolete. It's not that this year's computer suddenly becomes useless; rather that new software applications are developed which require more and more power. Nowhere is this more true than with computer games which are provided with ever more stunning graphics. However, serious applications such as Microsoft Office (word processor, spreadsheet, etc.) and Windows itself continue to demand more powerful machines as each new version is packed with additional features.

There are three ways to deal with this demand for more and more computing power:

- Settle for the computer system you've got. Ignore the latest versions of Windows and new software applications which may not run on your machine.

- Buy a brand new computer system every year or two and keep up to date. (Too expensive to consider for many people).

- Buy a computer which can be upgraded easily and cheaply.

Obviously the cheapest option is to settle for what you've got. Most common tasks such as Word Processing, Desktop Publishing, Accounts, Graphics, E-mail and surfing the Internet could be carried out perfectly well on machines built several years ago. However, if computing is your hobby, or you work in a business and deal with people having the latest technology, then you may want to keep up-to-date. After all, most experienced users would agree that Windows XP is much easier to use, more powerful and more reliable than Windows 95, for example.

This brings us to the third option, to buy a machine which can be upgraded cheaply. Peripheral units like the printer, keyboard and mouse can be swapped for improved models at any time. However, the important components inside of your computer's metal case should also be upgradeable. It's worth considering future *upgradeability* at the time of buying a new computer system.

If you're handy with a screwdriver you might have a go at this work yourself. Otherwise your local computer shop should be able to do the work in no time at all. If you have a good monitor, keyboard, mouse and printer all you need to consider upgrading are a few of the critical parts inside of the base unit. These are the processor, hard drive, memory and possibly one or two of the expansion cards.

Fitting a Faster Processor

This is mainly needed to run graphics programs quickly, such as simulations and games. Sometimes you can get away with simply plugging in a new processor, but you may also need to buy a new *motherboard* (the main circuit board inside of the computer). You should check before buying whether the processor can be swapped easily. Some older machines cannot be upgraded with a new motherboard because the computer case is not compatible.

Fitting a Bigger Hard Disc Drive

A simple upgrade, which many people can do for themselves is to fit a *bigger hard disc* drive. You may fill your existing drive with your collections of photographs or files of work. New programs tend to need far more hard disc space than the earlier versions. It may also be possible to leave your old drive in situ and simply add a second new drive.

Extra Memory

New versions of programs tend to be more memory hungry than earlier versions because of all the extra features that have been added. Shortage of memory causes excessive hard disc activity when you are not expecting it. This is indicated by the hard disc's light flashing. Lack of memory also causes the computer to run very slowly.

Adding *extra memory* is just a case of adding two or more additional memory modules known as SIMMs. These are small circuit boards containing banks of memory chips. It's a simple job to fit some new SIMMs into special clips in the motherboard.

Expansion Cards

Several other components are upgradeable because they consist of *expansion cards* or small circuit boards which plug into the motherboard. These cards include the *graphics card*, which controls the screen display, the *sound card* and perhaps an *internal modem* (if fitted). An example of an expansion card for an internal modem is shown on page 40.

All of these cards can be replaced by new, improved models, if desired. It's simply a case of removing the metal casing, disconnecting any cables, undoing a single screw and pulling the card out.

Please note that before removing the casing of your computer at any time, you should rid yourself of static electricity. This can be done by touching the frame of your computer or by touching some water pipes. You can also purchase special *anti-static earthing straps*, at a modest price, from most electrical shops.

The new card is pushed into place and the fixing screw and any cables are replaced before fitting the metal computer casing.

However, before buying a computer you should check with your supplier that there are spare slots for expansion cards. These might include a network card to connect your computer to another machine via a cable, a hand-held scanner whose circuitry may be on a card, and some additional *ports* or sockets for connecting devices to the back of the computer.

If you do want to keep up with latest trends, modern computers are generally upgradeable as previously described. However, you can delay the possible need to upgrade by buying the most powerful computer which you can reasonably afford. This really means the fastest processor, the biggest hard drive and the maximum memory.

Next

Issues to consider when buying a new computer and setting it up in your home are covered in the next chapter.

Getting Set Up

This chapter looks at the steps involved in buying a computer and getting it up and running in your own home. If you have read the previous chapters you should know if you can manage with a standard sort of machine, i.e. suitable for tasks like word processing and using the Internet. Such a basic machine will be readily available for a few hundred pounds. Alternatively if you or a member of your family is likely to be a "power user", perhaps handling a lot of large graphics files and photographs or playing the latest games, then you will need to buy a more powerful computer with a faster processor and probably costing upwards of a £1000.

Choosing a Supplier

There are several ways of obtaining a computer:

- Major stores with branches throughout the country.
- Mail order specialists.
- Small local businesses.
- Buying a second hand machine.
- Building your own computer from a kit.

Normally a basic computer system will consist of the base unit (tower or desktop), a monitor, a keyboard and a mouse. The base unit will always include the motherboard, processor, hard disc drive, floppy disc drive and CD drive. Some offers may also include a DVD drive for playing moving videos. The large chains have the advantage of bulk buying and can therefore offer very good prices.

If you go to one of the big stores they will often "bundle" a complete package to include a printer, modem and scanner for about £700 upwards, depending on the specification of the processor, hard disc, etc. This should also include Microsoft Windows (with Internet Explorer) and probably applications such as Microsoft Works (word processor, database, spreadsheet, etc.) to get you started.

Large stores and mail order companies also offer warranties, which may be on-site or on a return-to-base basis. Obviously the on-site option is more convenient. Return to base is not a good option for a computer system on which you depend for work or regular use. From my own experience, it can be extremely frustrating and expensive, as there may be post and packaging to pay in two directions. You may also have to spend hours on the telephone trying to find a person dealing with your machine. It's also not unknown for mail order companies to collapse while holding customers' money for machines not yet delivered.

I have had good experience dealing with small local computer builders. Obviously you need to choose a firm you can trust and if possible talk to previous satisfied customers. If the firm has been in business for a few years, this is a good indication. You may not get a complete package including a printer and scanner but you will get some other advantages. In a typical small business, you will be able to talk directly to the person who has built your machine and knows it thoroughly. If you know exactly what you want, the small business will probably build a machine tailored to your own specification.

If you do have problems it should only be a matter of returning the machine for perhaps a day or two. In the large store you may be talking to a sales person with no practical knowledge of computers.

Monitors are slightly different from the rest of the computer when it comes to repairs. If you take a faulty monitor to a computer specialist they often forward the monitor to a specialist repairer. This is often a person trained in the repair of televisions. If your monitor needs repair (and is out of warranty) it may therefore be cheaper to go directly to a specialist monitor/TV repairer. I have only had 2 monitor repairs in the last 5 years and as I keep a spare monitor (bought secondhand for £50) this has never been a problem.

Although you do hear horrendous tales, in practice most modern computers are very reliable and you will be unlucky if you have to return your machine. If treated with respect, I have found that most computers soldier on for years.

Another point to consider is the installation of the machine in your home. If you are not very mobile, you may need the supplier to deliver the machine to your house then set it up and get you started. This should include connecting to the Internet via your telephone socket.

When visiting a computer shop to buy a new machine, it is very easy to be bamboozled by the sales staff, who may have learned lots of impressive jargon but may not have very sound technical knowledge to support it. Before visiting the shop, have a look at a few magazines and get a feel for the latest prices and offers. Read Chapters 2 or 3 of this book so that you are familiar with the various parts.

Then you won't be baffled by terms such as RAM and "Pentium Processor", "kilobytes" and "gigabytes". Prepare a list of questions before leaving home - a good supplier will have no problem in giving you honest answers. A few ideas are given below.

Suggested Questions for Computer Suppliers

- What system would best suit your intended use of the computer?

- Is it easy to upgrade the computer in the future, with more memory, faster processor, bigger hard disc, more expansion cards?

- What guarantee is included with the machine and what does it cover?

- What are the arrangements for returning the machine and who pays for transportation?

- What is a typical turnaround time for repairs?

- What software is pre-installed on the machine - Windows, word processor, spreadsheet, etc.?

- What peripherals are included - printer, scanner, digital camera, etc.?

- Would the basic machine without these "free" peripherals be better value? Also, you may want a better printer, for example, than the one included in the package.

- Will the supplier deliver the computer and get it up and running in your home?

- Would they give you any free tuition to get you started?

After buying a new machine, keep all receipts and packaging in case the system has to be returned for repair.

Buying a Second Hand Machine

Computers depreciate rapidly and a recent secondhand system may be available for £200 or £300. However, computers become obsolete very quickly and unless your needs are very minimal I wouldn't recommend a second hand computer more than a year or two old. Unless you have personal knowledge of the background of a second hand computer, I think it is worth spending the extra money to buy a new machine. The way computers advance, even a new machine bought today will start to look a little out-of-date in a year or two's time.

Building Your Own Machine

This option is not nearly as difficult as it may seem. It's actually only a case of buying a kit and plugging together the main components, namely the motherboard, processor, memory, hard disc drive, floppy disc drive and CD-drive. All of the power cables are supplied already attached to the power supply unit in the computer's metal case. The cables are all different and cannot normally be fitted incorrectly.

If you are handy with a screwdriver and can spare the time you could certainly consider building you own computer. There are also lots of books on the subject. I have built two computers and both have given several years of reliable service. They have since been kept up-to-date by various upgrades to processors, memory and hard disc drives (rather like the woodman's axe which has had 3 new handles and 4 new heads).

However, you don't save a great deal of money building your own machine. What you do gain is a good knowledge about the workings of the machine and a great deal of personal satisfaction.

Creating the Right Environment

Before buying a new computer it's worth deciding where it's going to be set up in your home. If possible a separate small room such as a spare bedroom is ideal so that you can work without disturbance. Other people may use a special shed or summerhouse in the garden; I have converted part of a garage to create a small office as shown below.

If you are planning to use your computer for any sort of work or business, it may be worth installing some extra work surfaces. Also check with your insurance company that your house insurance is not affected. If you are using your computer for working from home, you may be able to claim the cost of any computer equipment, fixtures and fittings as capital allowances on your self-assessment tax form. If you are dedicating a room to your business or employment then you may be able to claim, for tax purposes, the cost of heating and lighting as a fraction of the total bill for the whole of your home.

Safety and Security Issues

If possible, have some extra power points installed in your room, by a competent electrician. A computer system with printer, scanner, speakers, etc., can easily require 6 or more power points. Connecting several plug adapters together is dangerous and might cause a fire, with possible consequences for any insurance claim you make.

You also need to make sure that the computer base unit and monitor have plenty of space around them, to prevent overheating and the possible risk of a fire. Install a smoke alarm near to the computer system. The increased risk of flooding in recent years must also be borne in mind when choosing a location for a new computer system.

Computers as a commodity are very popular with burglars. The computer system represents a big investment by any standards. What may not be realized is that the value of the hardware and software can easily be exceeded by the value of the data, in which you might have invested hundreds of hours of work. In the case of a small business, the loss of a computer system and all of the data may be devastating.

If your system is installed on the ground floor and visible from outside, it is asking to be stolen. I know of one case where a computer and then its brand new replacement were stolen from the same location next to a window, without the thieves ever entering the building. In a ground floor location the safest solution is to fit bars on the windows.

You might also mark your equipment with your post code, using a permanent marker pen, to deter thieves. Marking with an infra-red invisible pen may help in claiming your equipment if it's later recovered by the police.

Internet Access

You will also need a convenient telephone socket for connecting your machine to the Internet. The cheapest option is a telephone extension cable and socket and these are available from the large DIY stores. However, this ties up the telephone line so that other people can't use the 'phone while you are surfing the Internet. If you can afford it, installing a separate line is a better solution as this can be dedicated solely to the computer. As you will be billed separately for the dedicated line, you can also see the precise cost of your Internet and e-mail activities. This may be useful for tax purposes.

The latest *broadband* Internet connections (discussed later) allow the telephone to be used at the same time as the Internet connection, using a single telephone line.

Computer Furniture and Health Issues

The height of your desk and chair must allow you to work comfortably. Office chairs with adjustable seat height are available for about £30 upwards. Special computer tables, often called *workstations*, can cost over £100 while good second-hand office desks can be bought for as little as £30.

Long, unbroken hours at the computer can result in *RSI* or *Repetitive Strain Injury*. This can cause pain and serious injury in the muscles of the wrists, neck, back and shoulders. The risks of RSI can be reduced by making sure that your seating position allows a good posture, ensuring that your arms, wrists and thighs remain roughly level. Your back should be straight and you should not have to strain to reach forward. You are advised to move and stretch every few minutes and walk about, every hour, say.

Assembling the System

Assuming you have bought a new system and have identified a suitable location for the new machine, we can now consider putting the pieces together and starting the computer for the first time. At this stage it is probably best to concentrate on the basic system, i.e.

- Base unit
- Monitor
- Keyboard
- Mouse

Peripherals such as the modem and printer can be installed later when the basic system is working correctly. Don't switch any power on until the whole system is connected.

If you have bought a base unit in the tower configuration, you may find it easier to do an initial setting up on the work surface or desk. This is because if the tower unit is on the floor, the cables which connect into the back of the base unit can be difficult to fit for the first time, especially when you're lying on your back. Once you are familiar with the set-up you should have no trouble reassembling the cables with the tower unit on the floor.

Assembling the system mainly consists of plugging a few cables into the correct sockets on the back of the base unit. Fortunately most of these are designed so that you can't plug a cable into the wrong socket.

It's worth spending a few minutes familiarizing yourself with the connectors on the back of your base unit, as described on the following pages, before connecting the units together.

Connection Sockets on the Base Unit

This section looks at the various sockets or connectors on the back of a base unit, into which all of the peripheral devices such as the keyboard, monitor and printer are connected. Fortunately, most connectors are designed so that you cannot connect the wrong device.

The mouse and keyboard plug into two small round 6-pin female sockets known as *PS2 ports*. If you look closely at your machine you should see small icons or labels on the base unit to distinguish between the mouse port and the keyboard port. Take care to line the pins up with the holes in the port before gently pushing the plug home.

Some mice use what are known as the *serial ports*. These are two 9-pin D-type male sockets at the back of the base unit. They are also known as *COM1* and *COM2* and may be marked as such on the casing. One of the serial ports is often used to connect an external modem.

It's possible to buy adapters which allow the older serial port devices and connectors to work with the newer PS2 devices and connectors.

The large 25-pin D-type female connector on the back of the base unit is used to connect a "parallel printer" and is usually referred to as the *printer port*. Some scanners also connect to the printer port. This arrangement can be very ·inconvenient unless you fit a second printer port, allowing both printer and scanner to be used without having to swap cables.

New printers nowadays often use the USB port described on the next page.

Modern computers have two small rectangular female sockets known as the *USB ports*. These are a relatively new innovation and are designed to make peripheral devices easy to connect and set up. The USB ports are used to connect peripheral devices like printers, scanners and digital cameras, for example.

The main power lead into the computer attaches to the base unit through the 3-pin socket marked AC 230V as shown on the left. Also shown is the main switch for the power unit.

On the right above is the computer's cooling fan.

The remainder of the connectors and sockets for the various cables are on the outside end of the expansion cards, again at the back of the base unit, as shown below.

Expansion cards are described in the previous chapter. The cards fitted to individual machines vary according to what devices have been installed.

Referring to the bottom photograph on the previous page, the top two slots are filled by removable blanking plates. These can be removed to allow extra devices to be fitted. The purpose of the blanking plate is to prevent dust, etc., from entering the computer while a slot is not occupied.

Connecting the Monitor to the Graphics Card

The top connector shown on the previous page is a 15-pin D-type female socket. This is the connection for the monitor lead. Located behind the connector is the graphics card, which contains the circuitry controlling the screen display.

The monitor also has a power lead. On some computers this has its own plug, to be inserted into a power point on the wall. Other monitors take their power off the back of the computer using a power lead with a male connector.

The Sound Card - Attaching Speakers and a Joystick

The next card down on the photograph on the previous page is the sound card. The large 15-pin D-type female connector shown on the left of the photograph is the *Games Port*. The games port is used for attaching a joystick, used instead of a mouse for playing games. The small connectors on the right are for connecting various devices to the sound card, such as a pair of speakers and a microphone. The sockets are normally labelled, e.g. SPK and MIC, on the end plate of the sound card, though you may need a torch and magnifying glass to read them.

The Network Card

Below the sound card in the photograph on page 57 is the network card. This card is used to allow two or more computers to be connected together with cables. The different types of connector shown on the card are needed because there are various types of network cable. The network card is not normally fitted as standard and if you only have one computer you can forget about it for the time being. However, many homes and small businesses now have more than one computer and there are many advantages in connecting them on a network. I fitted this card in order to connect my two computers together for the purpose of exchanging data files, sharing a single Internet connection and backing up my work.

Connecting an Internal Modem

At the bottom of the group of expansion cards shown on page 57 is the end plate of an internal modem. The modem is used to connect the computer to the Internet.

The rectangular female socket is for the special lead which connects the modem to the telephone line. Another socket allows an ordinary telephone handset to be connected. This particular modem also has 3 additional sockets for a Web camera, speakers and a microphone.

As mentioned elsewhere in this book, *external* modems are also available. These have lights providing information about the modem's activities. The external modem is obviously easier to connect but adds to the clutter on your desk and is more vulnerable to theft or accidental damage.

If you remove an expansion card because a device is no longer needed, always replace it with a blanking plate to prevent dust entering the computer's internal components.

Connecting the Cables

You should now be familiar with the connectors on the back of the base unit. Do not at this stage plug in any of the power cables at the power points. Now connect the monitor, keyboard and mouse to their respective sockets on the base unit. It's important to make sure you have good light and take care to line up the pins in the connectors carefully before gently inserting the cable plugs. The pins are easily bent and this will render the component useless.

When you've connected all of the components, next plug the power leads into the power points. Switch on the power unit on the back of the computer. Next switch on the power points and press the main **ON/OFF** switch on the front of the base unit. Also press the switch on the front of the monitor. Green power indicator lights should be illuminated on the monitor and on the base unit.

The computer should start up with the screen initially displaying a lot of text giving technical details. Depending on which version of Windows you are running this may be followed by the Windows logo, then a Welcome message, then the Windows Desktop itself, shown below. There are many optional screen displays for the Windows Desktop - this is just one example from Windows XP.

The all important **start** button is shown on the bottom left of the previous screenshot. Also shown on the left-hand side are icons representing shortcuts to start the various installed programs.

If the Computer Fails to Start

If your monitor screen is blank, check that the green power indicator on the front is **ON**. Also check that the D-type connector on the monitor cable has been fitted correctly to the graphics card at the back of the base unit. If you didn't hear the hard disc spinning in the base unit (a bit like a jet engine starting up), check that the switch at the back of the base unit is in the **ON** position. Try switching on again using the main switch at the front of the base unit. If the computer still doesn't start up, switch off all power points and check all of the connections, before repeating the start-up test. If either the mouse or keyboard doesn't work, it's usually because the connectors have been incorrectly fitted.

Return to Base

If, after checking all of the connections, your computer still refuses to start up, it will have to be returned to your supplier. Unless you suspect the monitor to be faulty, it is easier to return just the base unit, especially in the case of a small local supplier. If you suspect the monitor to be faulty, perhaps you could borrow one from a friend to confirm your diagnosis. In the case of a system bought from a large company it will need to be parcelled up in its original packaging and returned to the company's repair department, possibly by parcel carrier. You might ask someone with more experience to check over the connections but do not allow anyone to remove the metal cover of your machine as this may invalidate any guarantee.

Shutting Down Correctly

Before discussing the actual use of the computer, it is appropriate at this point to discuss the correct procedure for shutting down and switching off the system. Failure to shut down properly can damage the data on your hard disc. If this happens, next time you start the computer it will carry out a lengthy and very inconvenient recovery procedure as it checks for any damage and attempts to repair it.

Surprisingly, the correct shut down procedure is initiated

by clicking the **start** button. Then you click **Turn Off Computer** on the bottom of the **start** menu. The following window appears:

The Turn Off Option

If you select **Turn Off**, a message will eventually appear telling you it is safe to switch off the computer. At this stage I normally switch off at the power points rather than switching off individual components like the monitor and base unit. If you switch a monitor off every night you may find a new switch is needed before very long.

The Hibernate Option

Not all computers support the **Hibernate** option shown on the previous screenshot. **Hibernate** is used for shutting down a computer after saving everything to your hard disc. For example, if you click **start, Turn Off Computer**, and **Hibernate** while your screen is displaying, say, a word processing document, the computer will shut down. However, next time you start the computer, the screen display will be exactly as you left it, with the document open where you finished working.

The Restart Option

Click the **Restart** button if you want to shut down and start up again straight away. For example, after making changes to the computer, like installing new software, the changes may not take effect until the computer has been restarted.

Starting a New Session

Next time you start a computing session it's just a case of switching on at the power points at the wall and pressing the **ON** switch on the front of the base unit. The computer should start up and display the main Windows screen showing the **start** button in the left-hand corner. (Unless you shut down with **Hibernate**, when it should restore your screen display and document exactly as you left it).

Tidying Up the Cables

After setting up your system, you may need to tidy up the leads and cables. These can be fastened together using plastic ties or possibly encased in plastic trunking available from electrical shops. If your mouse movement is restricted by the length of the cable, you can buy cable extensions for a few pounds. *Wireless* mice and keyboards allow total freedom of movement, similar to a cordless telephone.

Connecting a Printer

A printer is obviously essential in most computer systems. In this section we will connect an Epson Stylus inkjet printer, using Windows XP, the latest version of Microsoft Windows. The general method is the same for attaching any printer to a computer and is broadly similar for other hardware devices such as a scanner or an external modem.

Apart from the printer itself, you should be supplied with:

- A power cable to connect the printer to a power point.

- A *data cable* to connect the printer to the computer.

- Software on a CD or floppy disc to enable your computer to work with your particular model of printer. This software is known as a *printer driver*.

There are two main types of data cable used with printers:

- The *Centronics parallel printer cable* has been the standard for many years. One end of the parallel printer cable connects to the 25-pin D-type connector or printer port on the base unit, as discussed on page 56 of this book. The other end of the parallel cable connects to a 36-pin socket on the printer.

- The *USB cable* is a recent development for connecting various peripheral devices, in addition to printers. The USB cable connects the USB port on the printer to a USB port on the computer base unit. The USB ports are small rectangular slots as discussed on page 57 of this book.

Connecting the Cables

With all the power points switched off, connect the printer power cable and data cable.

Switch on the power supply for the printer and switch the printer on. The green power indicator light on the printer should be illuminated.

Switch on the power to the computer and start the computer by pressing the **ON/OFF** switch on the front of the base unit. The message **Found New Hardware** should appear in a balloon at the bottom right of the screen, as the computer automatically detects the new printer.

The **Found New Hardware Wizard** appears as shown below.

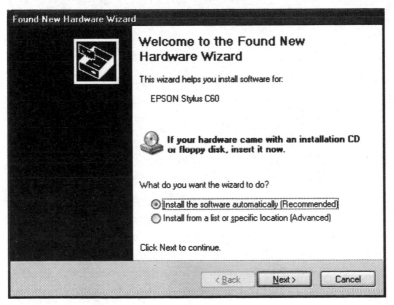

You are asked to insert the CD or floppy disc which came with your new hardware - in this case an Epson printer.

After inserting the CD, click the **Next** button as shown previously. The resulting window presents a list of choices of printer driver software in different languages.

In this example, there is not an English printer driver listed for Windows XP. However, there is one for Windows 2000 which is a close relative of Windows XP. Also there is a message (displayed on the window above), which states that **This driver is digitally signed**. This means the driver has been tested and approved for use with Windows XP. Some drivers will display the message **This driver has not been digitally signed!** If you decide to use such an unsigned driver you may later experience problems with the printer or other device. (Digital signing doesn't just apply to printers).

After choosing the printer driver, click **Next** and you are asked to click **Finish** to complete the installation.

Testing the Printer

You can see if your new printer driver software is installed on your computer by clicking the **start** button and then selecting **Printers and Faxes**.

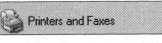

All of the printer drivers installed on your machine are displayed in their own window as shown below.

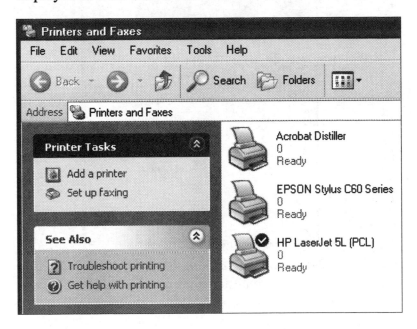

You can see the driver for the new Epson printer listed above. Also listed is my old printer, the **HP LaserJet 5L**. Notice that the LaserJet driver shown above is marked with a tick. This means it is set as the *Default* printer driver, i.e. the one which will be automatically used if printing from an application such as Microsoft Word.

Obviously if we now have an Epson printer physically connected to the computer, we should make the Epson driver the default printer driver. Move the cursor over the icon for the Epson driver shown previously. Clicking the *right* mouse button (in future referred to as "right clicking") brings up the menu shown below.

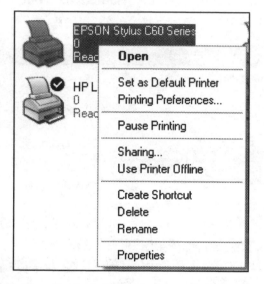

Now click **Set as Default Printer** to make the new Epson printer the one which is used automatically from applications.

Printing a Test Page

On the above menu, at the bottom is the **Properties** option. Clicking this brings up the **Properties** window. Make sure this window is displaying the **General** tab by clicking **General** at the top. At the bottom is a button marked **Print Test Page**. Clicking this button will show whether your new printer can print text and graphics correctly on paper.

You are asked if the test page printed correctly. If not click, **Troubleshoot...** as shown below, to try to solve the problem.

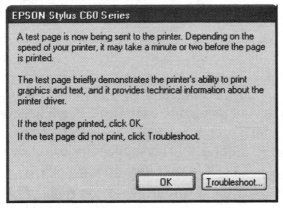

The **Printing Troubleshooter** shown below attempts to solve printing problems after you select from a list of common faults. Click the small circle (or *radio button*) to include one or more faults in the diagnosis of your printing problem.

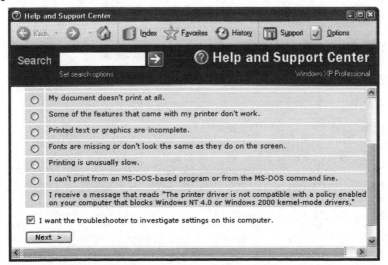

Using the New Printer

You will need to consult your printer manual for precise details about loading paper and fitting new ink cartridges (or toner cartridges in the case of laser printers).

If you have set the new printer as the *default*, as described on page 68 of this book, then this will be used automatically in any application such as a word processor. However, you can use any printer which is physically attached to your computer, even if it has not been set as the default printer. This is done by selecting the required printer driver from within an application, as follows.

In the application, select **File** and **Print...** from the menu bar. Now click the down arrow to the right of the default printer, in this example **HP LaserJet 5L (PCL)**, as shown below. Then, from the drop down menu, select the printer you wish to use. Click **OK** and printing should begin with the newly selected printer.

Introducing
Windows XP

What is Windows XP?

After you switch the computer on, it starts up and in a short while the screen displays the Windows Desktop with various icons, backgrounds and colours. During a session at the computer you might select a program from a menu, do some work such as typing a letter, save the letter on disc and print it out on paper. All of these tasks are controlled by a collection of software forming what is known as the *operating system*. Microsoft Windows in various editions has been the dominant operating system on personal computers for many years. Windows XP is the latest version of Microsoft Windows, now installed as standard on many new computers.

The operating system provides the environment in which we control and interact with the computer. It presents the menus from which we select commands or tasks, it controls the screen display and allows us to manage our document files and folders and to save and print our work. The operating system also controls peripheral devices such as scanners and modems and our connection to the Internet.

No matter what task we use our computer for - word processing, surfing the net, etc. - the operating system will be working in the background in overall control.

Windows XP also provides various tools for routine maintenance tasks and organizing your work. When you save a document, such as a letter, on your hard disc, the saved version is known as a *file*. The Windows operating system allows you to arrange your files into a system of organized folders (discussed later). Windows is also used for deleting any files of work which you no longer need. Windows XP includes its own *applications* software such as Internet Explorer. This is a Web browser, a program used for searching the Internet for information, such as bargain holidays or herbal remedies, for example. There is also a digital media player which allows you to turn your computer into an impressive music centre, with easily managed personal libraries of music and stereo sound.

The Evolution of Microsoft Windows XP

Windows XP is the latest in a family of Microsoft Windows operating systems, starting with Windows 3.0 and Windows 3.1, followed by Windows 95, Windows 98 and Windows Me. Business users were provided with separate versions of Windows, namely Windows NT followed by Windows 2000.

Windows 95, Windows 98 and Windows Me were primarily aimed at the home user and, while quite capable of running business programs, were also very suited to other areas of computing, such as games requiring sound and high quality graphics. Windows Me in particular introduced a new media player with facilities for copying and managing music CDs and for editing home videos.

Windows NT and Windows 2000, with their emphasis on business applications, were particularly strong on networking and security. In addition, being of a completely new design, they were more stable and reliable, not susceptible to "crashing" or locking up, as some users claimed of Windows 98, for example.

Windows XP is the result of a merger between the two Windows families, i.e. the home and business versions. In fact, there are two versions of Windows XP, known as Windows XP Home Edition and Windows XP Professional. The two versions are basically the same, both using the proven Windows NT technology at their core, known for its reliability and stability. The Professional Edition has additional features for network management and security in large organisations. Windows XP can also be installed on older machines, provided the machine meets certain performance criteria, described on the next page.

Moving Up to Windows XP

Hardware Requirements

As the Microsoft Windows operating system has evolved over the years it has become packed with more and more sophisticated features. This in turn demands ever more powerful computers in order to run at an acceptable speed. According to Microsoft, Windows XP requires a computer having the following *minimum* specification:

- PC with 300MHz or higher processor speed
- 64MB of RAM minimum but 128MB or higher recommended
- 1.5GB of available hard disc space
- CD-ROM or DVD drive

Please note that these are only *minimum* figures. A machine only just meeting this specification may work slowly - some people have said that 500MHz is the minimum processor speed to give acceptable performance.

If you have a computer on which you want to run Windows XP and the computer does not meet these minimum specifications, it may be worth upgrading, i.e. replacing one or more of the critical components listed above. This can be very much cheaper than buying a brand new machine. There will probably be several small businesses in your area specializing in building and upgrading computers and able to undertake the work at a reasonable price. If you are already running Windows 98, Windows 98 Second Edition, Windows Millenium (Me), Windows NT 4.0 or Windows 2000 Professional, you can buy an *upgrade* version of Windows XP. The upgrade version of the software is considerably cheaper than buying the full, standalone version of Windows XP.

Installing Windows XP

The installation process is started by inserting the self-"booting" Windows XP CD and responding to the on-screen instructions. The whole operation takes about an hour. If you are upgrading from an existing version of Windows, such as Windows Me, the installation may be interrupted while you are warned about compatibility issues. Since Windows XP is a new operating system, you may find there are problems of compatibility with some of your old hardware and software. In some cases you may be advised to remove software and perhaps re-install afterwards. In the case of incompatible hardware, you may need to visit the manufacturer's Web site to obtain modified *driver* software.

Alternatively, check the compatibility of your system before starting the installation by selecting **Check system compatibility** from the Windows XP CD, as shown below.

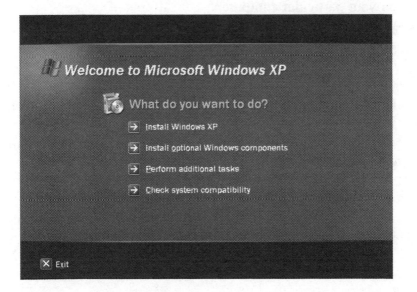

Product Activation

This is a new software feature intended to prevent, for example, a home or small business user buying one CD and installing it on several computers. This practice is known as *casual copying* and regarded as theft. Product Activation is aimed at the purchaser of a single Windows XP CD - it does not apply to large organizations buying multiple copies or to new computers supplied with Windows XP already installed.

The activation process relies on a unique *installation ID*. This is a number based partly on the *product key*, the string of 25 characters supplied on your Windows XP folder which you must type in during the installation process. The remainder of the installation ID is based on information automatically derived from the hardware components in your computer. Product Activation means your copy of the Windows XP CD can only be used to install Windows XP on your particular computer.

If you wish, activation can take place in response to a prompt during the Windows XP installation process. Otherwise, if you don't activate Windows XP straightaway, you can still use the software but only for the next 30 days. During this time you will be reminded to activate the software. After 30 days, Windows XP will cease to function, apart from the activation feature. During the 30 days there is an activation icon on the Windows XP screen.

The activation process can also be started by clicking:

start, All Programs, Accessories, System Tools and finally **Activate Windows** as shown on the menus below.

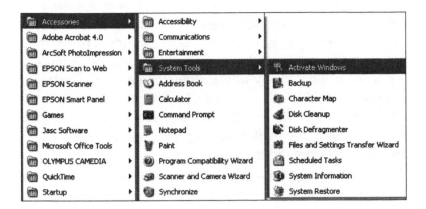

Activation can be carried out over the Internet or by a telephone call to Microsoft. The activation process is quite straightforward and only takes a few minutes. It does not require any personal information

If you make several changes to the hardware components of your computer, you may need to repeat the activation process at some point in the future. Product Activation is not to be confused with *registration* in which you supply details like your name and address, to ensure that you receive support and details of future Microsoft products.

A Brief Tour of Windows XP

The next few pages give an overview of some of the main features of Windows XP. Many of the topics are discussed in more detail later in this book. You will see that in addition to providing the software to run your computer, Windows XP also provides a wealth of software tools to maintain the system and carry out modifications. Windows XP also includes many *applications* of its own. These are programs which might otherwise be bought separately from alternative suppliers, and cover tasks such as browsing the Internet, sending e-mails, drawing and painting, editing text and working with digital media.

When you switch the computer on, you may notice that Windows XP starts up more quickly than earlier versions of Windows such as Windows 98. If the computer has been set up for several people to use, select your user name from the list of users, as shown below, and if necessary enter your password.

This gives you access to your own area of the computer, personalised with your preferred settings and giving secure access to your files.

The next screen to appear is the Windows Desktop, with the **start** button in the bottom left-hand corner and the Windows **TaskBar** along the bottom, as shown in the screenshot below. Apart from an icon for the **Recycle Bin** (discussed later), the Desktop on a new installation of Windows XP is completely clear. If you are upgrading from an earlier version of Windows, your previous Desktop icons will be retained.

It is also possible to place shortcut icons on the Windows XP Desktop to give quick access to frequently used programs and files. However, Windows XP reduces the need for shortcut icons by automatically placing frequently used programs and recent documents in the pop-up **start** menu shown below.

Entries can be deleted from the list of frequently used programs on the left of the panel.

For clarity, the top half of the previous **start** menu is shown enlarged below.

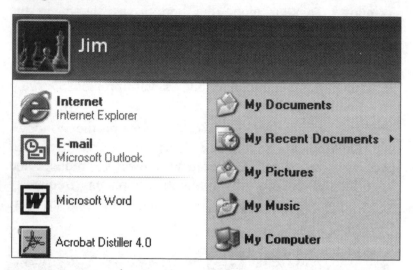

My Documents shown above right, is a special folder in which your work is saved "by default", unless you specify a different folder. (Creating your own folders and saving your work is discussed later). As shown below, apart from the documents and files you save, **My Documents** can also contain saved copies of pictures, music and e-books.

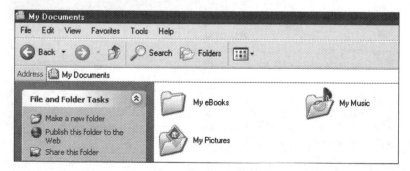

If you select **My Recent Documents** as shown on the previous menu, you are presented with a list of the latest documents you have been working on. Some recent documents are listed on the right of the following extract from the **start** menu.

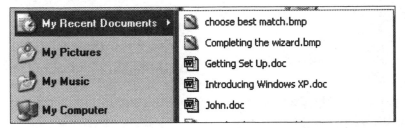

Please note that in this context a "document" is not just a letter or report in a word processor. Drawings and paintings, for example are also referred to as documents.

Also note that when a document is saved as a file, a filename is given by the user. For example, I have named a letter as **John** above. Then Windows has automatically added **.doc** to indicate that this is a word processing document. The document is further identified by the icon for a word processing document, shown above. Similarly a picture is saved with a different icon and the filename extension **.bmp,** which stands for Windows "bitmap". There are several other filename extensions for pictures and these are discussed later in this book.

The feature **My Recent Documents** provides a quick way of calling up a document you have recently been working on.

My Computer

Referring to the extract from the **start** menu shown below, **My Computer** listed in the right-hand panel is a very important tool used in the management of your computer

Clicking **My Computer** in the above **start** menu brings up the window shown below.

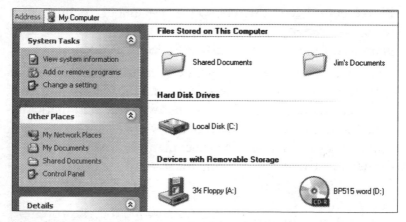

My Computer allows you to look at the various resources on your computer, such as disc drives and CDs. Amongst other things, you can carry out maintenance tasks such as cleaning up your hard disc by deleting unwanted files.

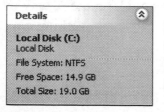

When you click on the icon for the hard disc drive as shown above, the panel at the bottom left of the **My Computer** window shows the amount of free hard disc space.

The Windows Explorer

The Windows Explorer displays all of the folders and files on your computer. It is one of the main ways to locate a piece of work (usually called a file). Then the document can be opened in the program which created it. The Windows Explorer lists all the resources of your computer (disc drives, folders, sub-folders, etc.) in a list down the left-hand side of the screen, as shown below.

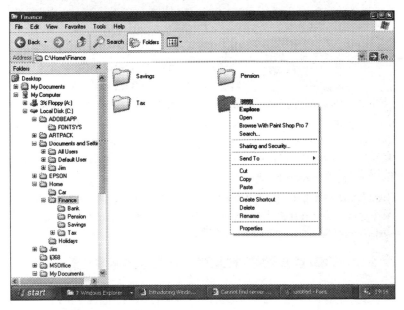

The right-hand panel above shows the contents of any folders you have opened. You can carry out a variety of management tasks on the folders and files listed in Explorer by right-clicking over the appropriate name or icon. This produces a menu as shown above on the right.

Amongst other things, the menu includes options to copy, delete, rename and create a shortcut to a file or folder from the Windows XP Desktop.

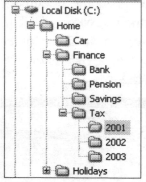

A *hierarchy* of folders is shown in the extract from the Windows Explorer on the left. Creating folders is discussed later. I have created a folder called **Home**, then within it there are sub-folders of **Car, Finance** and **Holidays**. Within the **Finance** folder there are sub-folders **Bank**, **Pension**, **Savings** and **Tax**. Within the **Tax** folder there are sub-folders for years **2001, 2002** and **2003**. Shown below is an example of a file saved in a sub-folder. The filename is **Letter about tax.doc** and it has been saved in the sub-folder **2001**. The full route to the file down through the various folders is known as the *path*. You can see the path given in the **Address** bar below, i.e. **C:\Home\Finance\Tax\2001. C:** refers to the hard disc drive, **Home** is my main folder and **Finance, Tax** and **2001** are the various sub-folders.

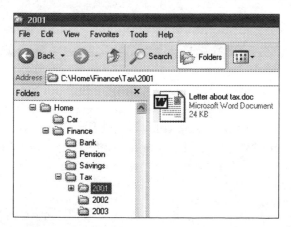

Launching Programs

We have seen that frequently used programs are automatically placed on the left-hand of the **start** menu for easy access. If desired, commonly used programs and files can also be launched from *shortcut icons* on the Windows XP Desktop, as discussed elsewhere in this book. The main bulk of your programs, however, are launched by selecting **start** and **All Programs**, as shown below.

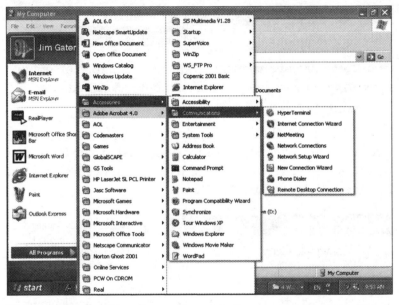

The programs listed on the **All Programs** menu shown above are a mixture of the software applications you have installed (such as your favourite word processing or painting package) together with a vast range of software applications and tools provided by Windows XP. When Windows is first installed from the CD you can select which components to include. Any components not included can always be added later.

Many of Windows XP's own programs are reached from the **Accessories** menu shown above. These include the Windows **Paint** program, **Windows Explorer** (discussed shortly) and the **Notepad** and **WordPad** text processors for creating and editing simple documents.

Menu options with a right-pointing arrow lead to further menus such as the **Communications** menu off the **Accessories** menu shown previously and below.

The **Communications** menu contains a number of options for setting up your Internet connections, discussed later.

Accessibility Features

Windows XP allows you to set up a number of **Accessibility** features to help with vision, hearing and mobility. These are listed after selecting **Accessibility** from the **Accessories** menu.

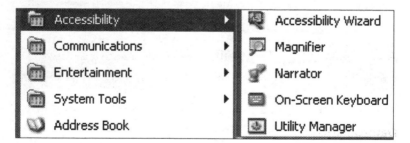

Please note that a **Wizard** in this context, as in the case of the **Accessibility Wizard** above, is a program which guides you through the process of setting up a piece of hardware or software. The **Accessibility** features are discussed in more detail shortly.

The Windows Media Player

The **Windows Media Player**, which is launched from **start** and **All Programs**, allows you to create and manage your own music CDs and edit home movies.

You can copy your CDs onto your hard disc and then compile playlists of your favourite records. These can be played in the background while working at the computer. The Windows Media Player has many other features and these are discussed in a separate chapter later in this book.

System Tools

An important feature within the **Accessories** menu is **System Tools**, shown below. This menu includes a number of maintenance tools intended to keep your computer running efficiently, such as **Disk Cleanup**, and **Disk Defragmenter**.

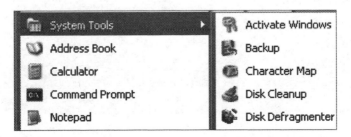

The Control Panel

This is an essential component of Windows XP, used (amongst other things) for altering settings and adding and removing new hardware and software. The **Control Panel** can be launched by clicking its name in the previously shown **start** menu. Alternatively click **Change a setting** in the **System Tasks** menu on the left of the **My Computer** window. The **Control Panel** opens in the **Category View** shown below. This view shows the tasks, under broad headings, which can be performed using the **Control Panel**.

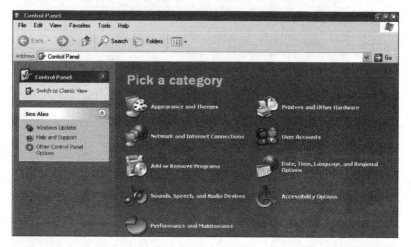

Selecting, for example, **Performance and Maintenance** as shown above, leads to some more specific tasks for you to choose from, as follows:

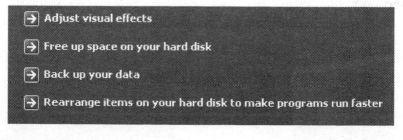

The Control Panel in Classic View

Earlier versions of Windows showed the Control Panel as a set of icons representing the various tools. This arrangement, now known as Classic View, is still available in Windows XP. Classic View can be selected by clicking the option **Switch to Classic View** in the Control Panel in Category View shown previously.

With the Control Panel in Classic View, as shown above, changes are made to settings after double-clicking the appropriate icon. For example, double-clicking the **Display** icon allows you to change all of your screen colours and to select a *screen saver*.

A screen saver is a display which occupies your screen if the computer is not used for a few minutes. The screen saver presents a constantly changing pattern or picture. This is to prevent burning of the monitor which might occur if the display remained fixed for a long time. There is a choice of screen savers within Windows XP and many others are available in all sorts of designs.

Windows Update

Both views of the Control Panel also give access to **Windows Update**. Clicking this option connects your computer to the Internet (if your machine already has a modem set up to connect to the Internet.) Here you are given the opportunity to  download the latest upgrades available for the Windows software installed on your computer. (*Downloading* means transferring files, i.e. programs and data, from the Internet to your computer).

Deleting Files - The Recycle Bin

This is a container for your deleted files and folders. When you delete a file by pressing the **Delete** key over the file name in the Windows Explorer or My Computer, the file is initially sent to the Recycle Bin. Files and folders in the Recycle Bin are still taking up space on your hard disc.

The **Recycle Bin** is launched by double-clicking its icon on  the Windows XP Desktop. From here the files can be permanently deleted. Alternatively, files in the **Recycle Bin** which have not yet been permanently deleted can still be restored to their original location on the hard disc.

That completes the tour of the main features of the Windows XP operating system. The next chapter looks at the different parts of a window and how we use them.

Working with Windows

Windows are rectangular boxes on the screen, used to frame the current task. A window might contain, for example:

- A document in an *application* such as a word processor, drawing program or a spreadsheet.
- A display of discs and folders in My Computer or the Windows Explorer.
- The set of icons or a list of tasks in the Control Panel, used for setting up hardware and software.

Although windows are used for such diverse purposes, in general they contain the same basic components. Shortly we will look at the make-up of a typical window. However, since the mouse plays a central role in the operation of windows, let's look at the use of the mouse in some detail.

You can tailor the mouse and pointer to work in the way you prefer. Select **start**, **Control Panel** and make sure you are displaying **Classic View**. Double-click the mouse icon, shown on the right, to make various adjustments to the way the mouse and pointer work. These include swapping the functions of the left and right button and altering the double-click speed.

Mouse Operations

Click

This means a single press of the left mouse button. With the cursor over an icon or screen object, a click will cause, for example, a command from a menu to be carried out or a folder to open.

Double Click

This means pressing the left mouse button very quickly twice in succession. This is often used to carry out operations such as starting a program from an icon on the Windows Desktop. Folders can be set to open with either a single or double click (discussed later).

Right Click

Pressing the right button while the pointer is over a screen object is a quick way to open up additional menus relating to the object. For example, if you right-click over the **start** button on the Taskbar, a menu appears giving, amongst other things, a quick way to start the Windows Explorer.

| **Open** |
| Browse With Paint Shop Pro 7 |
| Explore |
| Search... |
| Properties |

Dragging and Dropping

This is used to move objects about the screen. This includes moving files and folders into different folders or disc drives. Click over the object, then, keeping the left button held down, move the mouse pointer (together with the object) to the new position. Release the left button to place the object in its new position. Dragging is also used to resize windows and graphics on the screen.

Windows in Detail

The parts of a window can be illustrated using My Computer or the Windows Explorer. **My Computer** is selected from the **start** menu. The Explorer can be launched by *right-clicking* over the **start** button and then clicking **Explore** on the menu which appears.

In this example I have clicked on a folder called **Home** and then on a sub-folder called **Holidays**.

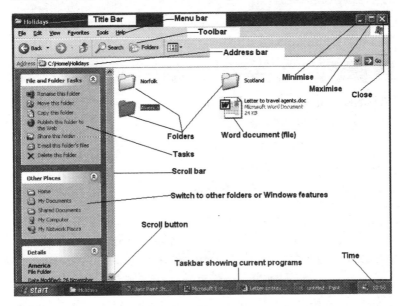

Similar windows are used for different purposes in Windows XP. For example, if you were word processing in Microsoft Word your document on the screen would be contained in a window with a Title Bar, Menu Bar, Toolbar and Taskbar. Both vertical and horizontal Scroll Bars may be displayed at different times.

You can choose which Toolbars are displayed by switching them on or off after selecting **View** and **Toolbars**.

Next, consider the three heavily used buttons in the top right of the screen, Maximize, Minimize and Resize.

The Maximise Button

Click this to make the window fill the entire screen.

The Minimise Button

Click this to reduce the window to an icon on the Taskbar at the bottom of the screen as shown below.

Letter to hotel.doc -...   untitled - Paint   Microsoft Excel - Bo...

The Taskbar above shows that the computer is currently running three programs. These are:

- A document, **Letter to hotel.doc**, open in Word.
- A drawing in Microsoft Paint.
- A spreadsheet in Microsoft Excel

Click the icon on the Taskbar to restore a minimised window back to its original size. The icon on the Taskbar can also be used to minimise an open window.

The Restore Button

After a window has been maximised, the Maximise Button is replaced by the Restore Button shown right. Clicking this reduces the window to its original size.

Closing a Window

To shut down the current window, click the Close Button, marked with a cross, in the top right-hand corner of the screen.

Resizing a Window

You can change the size of a window by dragging arrows on each of the four sides and in the corners of the window. Move the mouse pointer over the border until the arrows appear. Then drag the border to the required size.

The Menu Bar

The Menu Bar is a list of words across the top of the window starting with **File, Edit** and **View**, etc. For example, the menu bar from the Microsoft Word program is shown below. The icons underneath the Menu Bar are the Toolbar.

A single click of a word on the Menu Bar reveals a drop-down menu, such as the **File** menu illustrated. Then the required command is executed, again with a single click. Clicking the two small arrows at the bottom of the drop-down menu shown on the right extends the list of options.

Windows programs in general have a similar Menu Bar with the options **File, Edit** and **View**, etc., although there are some differences in individual programs.

The row of icons under the Menu Bar is part of the Standard Toolbar in Word. Similar Toolbars appear in other programs.

Allow the pointer to dwell over an icon. After a second or so a note appears describing the function of the icon. For example, when you hover over the scissors icon, the **Cut** command is revealed as shown on the left. This is used to delete or cut a piece of text in a document. (First you must highlight or select the required text by dragging with the mouse).

You can switch various toolbars on and off after selecting **View** and **Toolbars** from the Menu Bar as shown in the following example from Word.

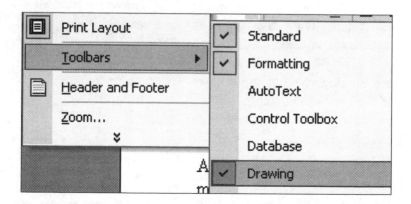

Displaying Two or More Windows at a Time

When two or more programs are running at the same time, normally only one of them is seen in a window on the screen. The others are minimised on the Taskbar at the bottom of the screen as shown previously on page 94.

Microsoft Windows allows two or more windows to be displayed simultaneously by a *tiling* arrangement. Tiling is achieved after *right-clicking* on an *empty part* of the Windows Taskbar at the bottom of the screen. This brings up the menu shown on the right. For example, selecting **Tile Windows Vertically** when running Word and Excel, produced the following result. Windows can also be tiled horizontally and the same method can be used for 3, 4 or more windows.

Toolbars   ▶
Cascade Windows
Tile Windows Horizontally
Tile Windows Vertically
Show the Desktop
Task Manager

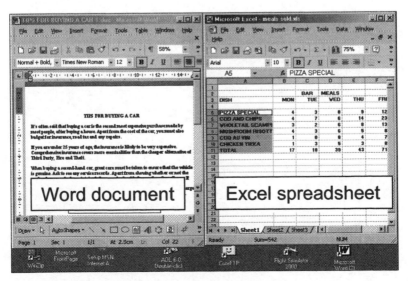

Word document   Excel spreadsheet

The **Cascade Windows** option shown in the menu on the previous page has the effect of arranging the windows on top of each other in layers, but with the Title Bar of each window clearly visible. Clicking on the Title Bar of a window brings that window to the top layer. Please note that windows currently minimised on the Taskbar are not included in any tiling or cascading arrangements.

Dialogue Boxes

Whereas the windows discussed previously contain running programs and folders, *dialogue boxes* (as shown below) usually require the user to enter information or specify settings. (Microsoft Windows provides *default* settings and names which will usually suffice until you are ready to insert your own settings.)

Dialogue boxes appear after you select a menu command which ends in an ellipsis (**...**) such as **Save As...** and **Print...**. The **Print** dialogue box shown below contains many of the most common features of dialogue boxes.

The white circles under **Page range** on the previous dialogue box are known as *radio buttons*, switched on or off with a single click. Only one of a group of radio buttons can be switched on at a given time.

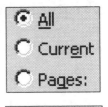

The white squares next to **Print to file**, **Manual duplex** and **Collate** are known as *check boxes*. Any number of check boxes can be switched on or off at a given time.

Clicking the *down arrow* on the right of a horizontal bar reveals a *drop-down menu* of choices, such as several printers, as shown below.

HP LaserJet 5L (PCL)
Acrobat Distiller
Acrobat PDFWriter
EPSON Stylus C60 Series
Generic PostScript Printer
HP LaserJet 5L
HP LaserJet 5L (PCL)

Some dialogue boxes have a *text bar* which allows you to type in your own words, such as a file or folder name. For example, when you select **Save As...** from the **File** menu, the **Save As...** dialogue box appears. This includes an icon to create a new folder, shown on the right. Click this icon and then enter a name for the new folder in the text box which appears, as shown below.

New Folder

Name: OK   Cancel

Creating a Shortcut Icon on the Desktop

To provide a shortcut icon on the Desktop for any of your programs, from the **start** menu, select **All Programs**. *Right-click* the name or icon for the program and click **Send To**. Now select **Desktop (create shortcut)** to place an icon on the Windows Desktop.

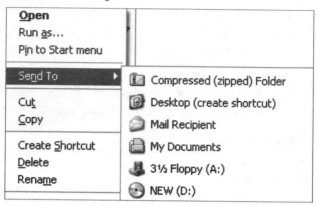

From now on the program can be started by double-clicking the icon on the Desktop. You can also create shortcuts on the Desktop to frequently used files and folders after right-clicking the file or folder in Explorer or My Computer and using **Send To** and **Desktop (create shortcut)**. As shown in the extract from my Desktop below, there are shortcut icons for, (from left to right), the Paint Shop Pro image editing program, the Google Internet search engine, my e-mail inbox and a word processing document.

Help for Users With Special Needs

Microsoft Windows XP contains a number of features to help with the following impairments:

- Vision
- Hearing
- Mobility

The features provided in Windows are limited and some users with special needs may require more specialised accessibility software. However, there are many useful tools included in Windows XP, to assist users with impaired sight, hearing or mobility and these are described on the following pages.

The Accessibility features are launched by selecting **start**, **All Programs**, **Accessories** and **Accessibility**.

Accessibility	▶	🔍	Accessibility Wizard
Communications	▶	💬	Magnifier
Entertainment	▶	🖊	Narrator
System Tools	▶	⌨	On-Screen Keyboard
Address Book		📋	Utility Manager

The next section looks at the five **Accessibility** options, shown in the right-hand panel above.

The Accessibility Wizard

A wizard is a program which leads you through a series of interactive screens. The user makes selections from various choices before clicking **Next** to move on to the next screen. Wizards are frequently used in Microsoft Windows for setting up new hardware and software.

Start the **Accessibility Wizard** by clicking **start, All Programs, Accessories** and **Accessibility**. First you see the **Accessibility Welcome Screen** and on clicking **Next** you are given the option to select a larger text size.

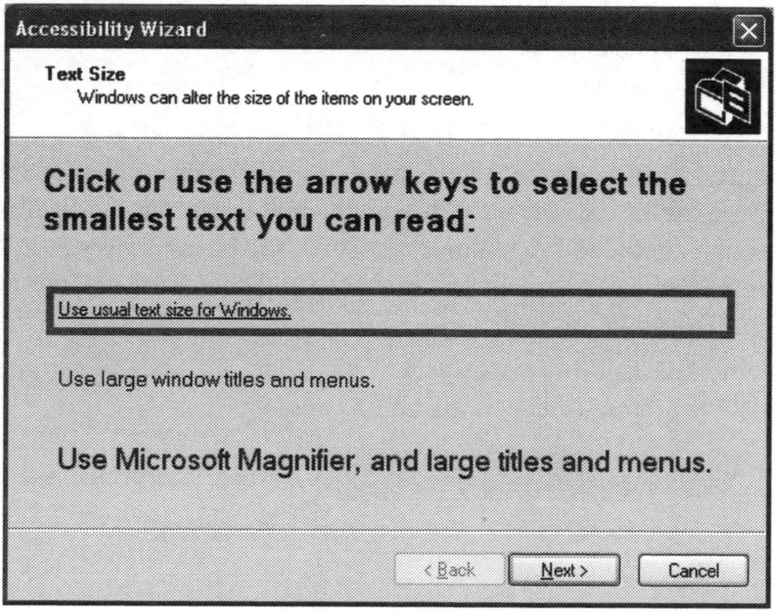

Further dialogue boxes in the wizard allow you to increase the text size which appears in windows title bars and also to increase the size of scroll bars.

Then you are asked to specify your own special needs, by ticking the check boxes for conditions which apply to you.

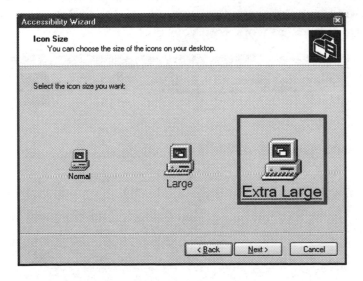

The Acccssibility Wizard then proceeds in one of several ways, depending on the ticks you have placed in the above check boxes. For example, if your vision is impaired, the option to display large icons is presented, as shown below.

Another dialogue box allows you to select a high contrast colour display and this is followed by a box giving a choice of various colours and sizes of mouse cursor.

If you find using a mouse difficult, the numeric keypad on the right of the keyboard can be used instead. For example, using this option, the cursor can be controlled by the arrow keys, a mouse click is replaced by pressing **5** and double clicking is replaced by +. Finally a dialogue box appears allowing you to swap the function of the left and right mouse buttons, to work with your preferred hand.

After completing all of the dialogue boxes, click **Finish** to leave the Accessibility Wizard. Please note that you can also set the **Accessibility Options** without using the Wizard. First enter the **Control Panel** from the **start** menu. Make sure the **Control Panel** is in **Classic View**. If the **Control Panel** is currently in **Category View**, click **Switch to Classic View** from the top left-hand corner of the **Control Panel**.

Now double-click the icon for **Accessibility Options**. The following dialogue box opens. A series of tabs (**Keyboard, Sound, Display,** etc.) give access to many further options.

The Magnifier

This feature enables the person with impaired vision to enlarge different areas of the screen, as required. The Magnifier is started by clicking **start**, **All Programs**, **Accessories**, **Accessibility** and **Magnifier**, as shown below.

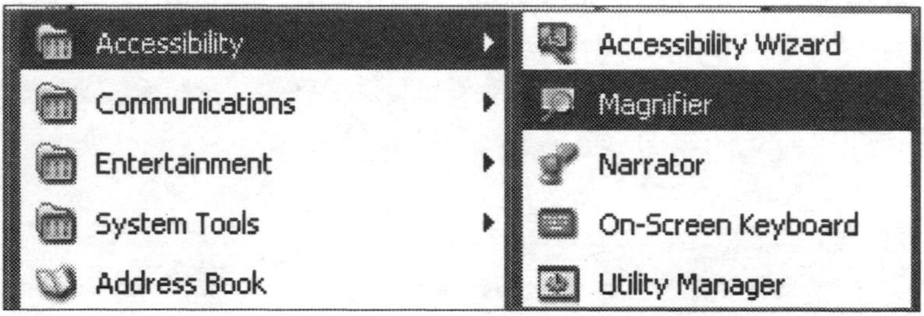

A settings dialogue box also appears, giving you the option to change the magnification level in the range 1 to 9.

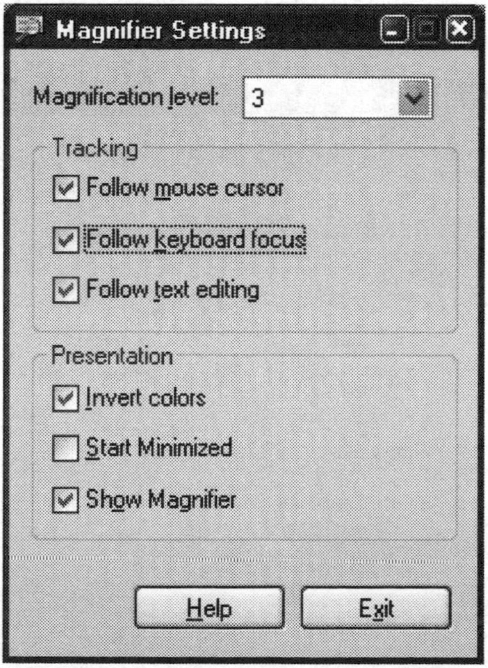

You are presented with a note stating that the Magnifier is intended for users with slight visual impairment. Those with more serious visual problems will need a program with higher functionality.

Note in the dialogue box on the previous page, you can set the magnifier to follow the mouse cursor and the keyboard focus. You can also invert colours to make the screen easier to read. The magnifier appears in its own window above the normal screen. As you move about the normal screen, the magnifier tracks the cursor or keyboard and displays the local text and graphics enlarged, as if viewed through a magnifying glass.

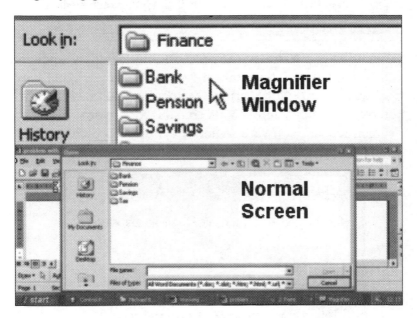

The Narrator

If your computer is fitted with speakers, the Narrator can read out the text in menus and describe features such as buttons in dialogue boxes. The Narrator can also read out the letters and keys pressed as you type them into a document. To start the program, select **start**, **All Programs**, **Accessories**, **Accessibility** and **Narrator**.

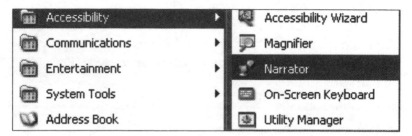

After clicking **Narrator**, an introductory window appears informing you that **Narrator** only works in English and may not work well with certain software. The user is also referred to the Microsoft Web site for details of other "screen reader" software. After clicking **OK** a dialogue box appears allowing the various options to be set in Narrator.

The On-Screen Keyboard

This feature is intended for anyone with mobility problems, who finds it difficult to handle a normal keyboard. The **On-Screen Keyboard** is launched from **start, All Programs, Accessories, Accessibility** and **On-Screen Keyboard**.

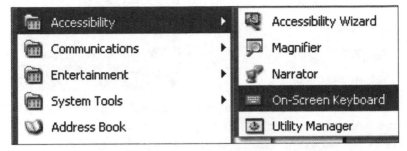

The on-screen keyboard is operated by a mouse or some other pointing device. The cursor is moved over the required letter and the mouse is clicked, causing the letter to appear on the page at the current cursor position.

The Utility Manager

The **Utility Manager** is started from **start**, **All Programs**, **Accessories**, **Accessibility** and **Utility Manager**.

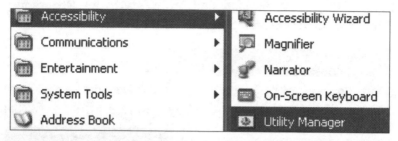

A dialogue box appears showing, within a single window, the special needs programs which are currently running. Here the programs can be started, stopped or configured.

The previous pages describe the special needs features provided free within Windows XP. The Microsoft Web site gives details of additional specialist software and hardware resources to help users with a range of impairments.

Introducing Microsoft Works

Introduction

Microsoft Works is a popular software package which includes just about everything you need to make good use of your computer. Even if you're using a different package, such as Microsoft Office or Lotus SmartSuite, the methods described in this chapter are still relevant.

If you've just bought a new PC, perhaps for accessing the Internet or sending e-mails to your friends and family, you may well have a copy of Microsoft Works already sitting on the hard disc inside your computer. It's such a popular and useful software package that it's often "bundled" with new computers from the large suppliers. At the time of writing I am using Microsoft Works Version 7, although many new machines are still being supplied with Works Version 6 installed.

If Works has already been installed on your computer, you should see its icon displayed on the Windows desktop, as shown on the right. Alternatively you can buy the Works package separately from any of the well-known high street suppliers or mail order companies.

Installing Software - Microsoft Works

It's a very simple task to install Microsoft Works or any other Windows software. The general method is the same whatever the piece of software being installed. This includes copying a lot of files from the installation CD onto your hard disc. The installation process usually places an icon for starting the software on the Windows Desktop. Commands to start the various programs will also be placed in the **All Programs** menu accessed from the **start** button.

The Contents of a Software Package

When you buy a package such as Microsoft Works, you will normally receive a box containing the installation CD and a user manual. Nowadays the user manual is often a very slim volume just intended to get you started. A more comprehensive manual may be provided on the CD. This can either be displayed on the screen or printed out on paper. Most software also provides an on-screen **Help** menu which can be viewed while a program is running.

There is often a guarantee registration card in the package, to be returned to the manufacturer. It is also common for you to be given the opportunity to register your purchase of the software as part of the installation process. To achieve this, the computer will be connected to the Internet so that you can enter your details on-line.

During registration, you can choose (or refuse) to be sent details of the company's latest upgrades to the software and other products which may be of interested. Registering the product may also entitle you to free telephone support for an initial period after which support must be paid for.

The address of an Internet Web site giving answers to FAQs (Frequently Asked Questions) is usually provided. Some packages include a Product Key. This is a long string of letters and numbers which must be entered before the software can be installed. This code is normally stuck on a label on the CD case and should be kept in a safe place. The code will be needed if you ever have to re-install the software at a later date. For example, if the original installation should become corrupted or your hard disc has to be reformatted (wiped) for some reason.

The Installation Process

Modern programs are easy to install and users can do the job themselves without seeking expert help.

Start the computer and make sure no programs (other than the Microsoft Windows operating system itself) are running. In particular some anti-virus programs can cause problems during software installation and these programs should be shut down or disabled.

Place the CD in the drive. The CD should *autoboot*, i.e. start up on its own. First there should be a Welcome screen, including a request for you to wait a few minutes.

Then you are given the name of a folder into which the software is to be installed on your hard disc. This includes the full path down through the folder system on the hard disc or **C:** drive.

For example:

C:\Program Files\Microsoft Works\

If for any reason you wish to install the software in a different folder, click the **Change** button showed on the next page. I always click **Next** to accept the folder specified by the software.

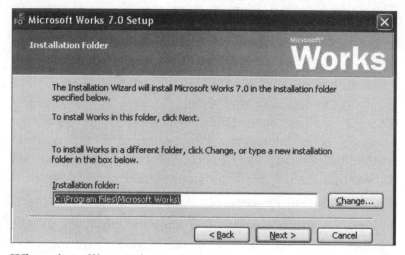

When installing Microsoft Works, after clicking **Next** a dialogue box presents three installation options, **Complete**, **Basic** and **Minimum**. It is recommended that you choose the **Complete** installation, assuming you have the necessary 190 megabytes of free space on your hard disc. Otherwise you can choose one of the smaller installations which will obviously have some of the less essential features omitted.

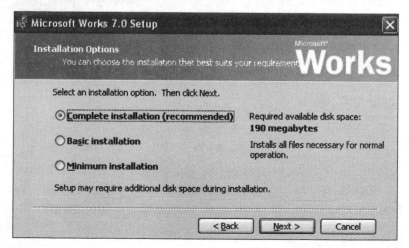

Clicking the **Next** button presents another window which asks you to wait while the software is installed. During the installation various features of the Works software are described and a **Status** bar keeps you informed of progress, as shown below.

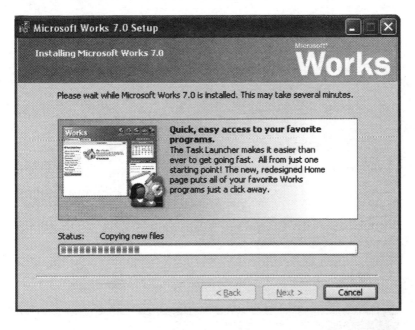

Finally you click **Next** and are told **You're done!** Click **Finish** to complete the installation. You should now have an icon for the software on the Windows Desktop and entries for your new software in the **All Programs** menus off the **start** menu.

📁 Microsoft Works ▶	📝 Microsoft Works Word Processor
📝 Microsoft Works Task Launcher	📊 Microsoft Works Spreadsheet
	📇 Microsoft Works Database

Using Microsoft Works

When you double-click on the Microsoft Works icon on the desktop you are presented with the **Task Launcher** (also accessible from **start** and **All Programs**). This displays the various features which make up the Works package.

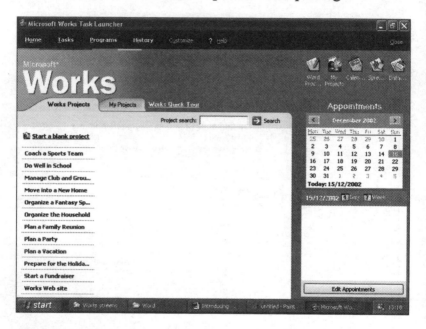

You can see icons for the main programs along the top right-hand corner of the screen. These are the word processor, spreadsheet and database, discussed later. Also listed are the **Calendar** and an icon called **My Projects**. On the right of the **Task Launcher** is an appointments list for the current month. If you click the **Edit Appointments** button at the bottom right of the **Task Launcher** a **Calendar** opens up enabling you to enter new appointments or edit existing ones.

Down the left-hand side of the **Task Launcher** there is a list
of projects that you may wish to undertake. For example,
Plan a Family Reunion, as shown in the extract below.

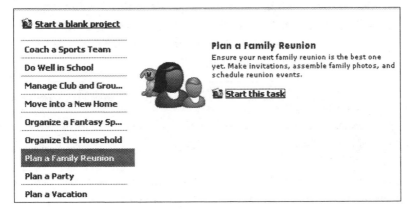

If you click **Start this task** as shown on the right above, you
are presented with a **To Do List** giving various tasks needed
to complete the project.

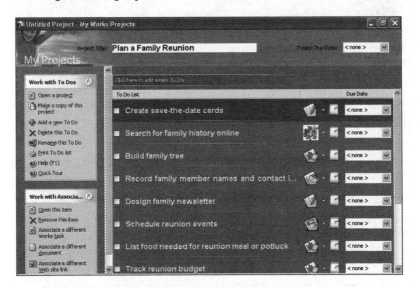

Clicking the icon on each of the entries in the **To Do List** shown on the previous page leads to various programs set up to help with specific tasks. For example, **Search for family history online** connects to a genealogy Web site on the Internet. **Build family tree** shown on the previous page open up the Works spreadsheet, with headings for various ancestors already mapped out.

A1		" Five Generation Family Tree			
	E	F	G	H	
6					
7	Grandfather's Name		Great Grandmother's Name		Great-Great
8	Born: Place / Date		Born: Place / Date		Born / Died
9	Died: Place / Date		Died: Place / Date		Great-Great
10	Married: Place / Date				Born / Died

Another item on the **To Do List** allows you to **Create invitations**. These are ready-made greetings cards, already containing a graphic and some text. The idea is that you customize the text to suit your personal requirements.

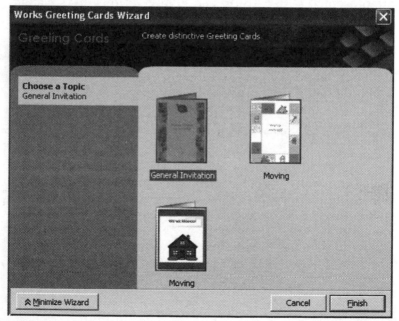

Clicking the **Tasks** tab at the top of the **Task Launcher** shown below presents a list of more specific tasks than the **Projects** section just discussed.

For example, selecting **Newsletters and Flyers** and **Start this task,** as shown above, opens the **Works Newsletter Wizard**. This gives a choice of several different newsletter designs. After selecting the design and clicking **Finish**, the **Works Word Processor** opens up with a template for your chosen design already in place. All you have to do is add your own headings and text to the template, as shown below.

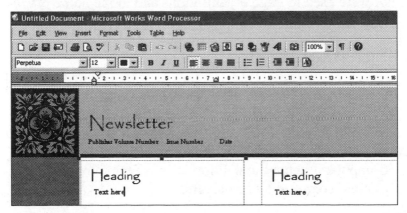

The **Task** and **Projects** features just discussed provide templates and wizards for a large range of possible activities. In addition, Works has a **Programs** feature which gives a menu for all of the Works programs and a **History** feature which lists all of the files you have created.

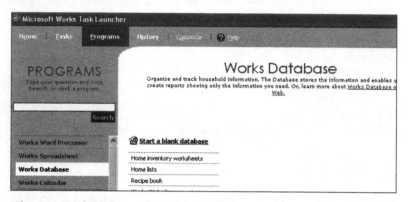

That completes an overview of the ready-made templates and wizards provided in Microsoft Works to help with specific tasks and projects. The next few chapters concentrate on the "content free" software which allows you to create your own documents and files from scratch.

Microsoft Works includes all of the most important software used in large organisations and in the home office, namely:

- The Word Processor
- The Spreadsheet
- The Database

Once you have learned how to use these programs you are well on the way to becoming "computer literate". In fact these three programs are at the heart of the popular CLAIT (Computer Literacy and Information Technology) course, widely recognized by employers.

Microsoft Works is an example of *integrated* software, since it embraces, in one package, a number of important programs which are also sold and installed separately. As mentioned previously these are the word processor, spreadsheet and database. These programs are essential for running a small business or performing a range of useful tasks for the home user.

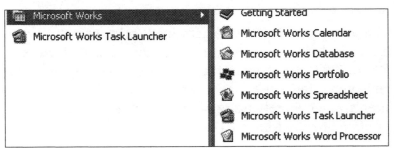

If you are not familiar with the functions of the word processor, spreadsheet or database, brief outlines of their roles are given later in this chapter.

A major advantage of integrated software like Microsoft Works (and its larger relative Microsoft Office) is the common "user interface". This means that all of the programs in the suite have the same look and feel; perhaps more importantly, any work you produce in one program can easily be transferred to another. So, for example, you might produce a set of accounts in the spreadsheet program then incorporate them into a report typed in the word processor. If you were to buy a word processor program from one company and a spreadsheet from another, you might encounter compatibility problems when you attempt to transfer documents or files between programs.

Another advantage of Microsoft Works is the price - it can be bought for well under £100. Although it may not have some of the more exotic features of packages costing hundreds of pounds, a typical home or small business user should find Works more than adequate for most general computing needs. Indeed, it has been found that most of us only utilize a small fraction of the features when using modern programs such as Microsoft Word.

The enhanced version of Microsoft Works, namely Works Suite, includes several extra programs such as Microsoft Word 2002, the program favoured by large organizations and professional users all over the world. This book has been typeset entirely using Microsoft Word 2002, ready for printing directly from a CD.

In fact the ordinary user will probably notice little difference between the software used in the Microsoft Works package and those in the more expensive packages such as Microsoft Office. For example, the menu bars from the Microsoft Works and Microsoft Word word processors are remarkably similar, as shown below.

The Role of the Word Processor

The word processor is a program used for the production of text-based documents. After launching the program you are presented with a blank screen into which you begin typing your document.

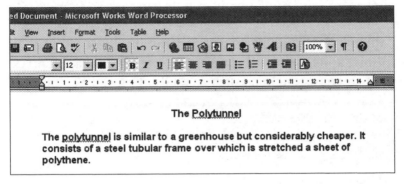

Any mistakes can be corrected on the screen and saved on a floppy or hard disc before being printed on paper. There are numerous additional features such as the ability to use different styles of lettering and page layout as well as extra tools like a spelling checker and a thesaurus. The word processor may be used for tasks ranging from a simple letter to a report including graphs and pictures or a flyer including pictures and text in newspaper-style columns. After entering the text, the document is saved on the hard disc. If you want to give a copy of a document to a friend to view or edit on their computer then it can be saved on a removable floppy disc or a CD.

A great deal of time is saved by the fact that documents can be stored on disc then retrieved and used again with only minor alterations, such as the date. This saves retyping the whole document, since, unlike the typewriter, alterations made on the word processor are invisible.

The Role of the Spreadsheet

The spreadsheet greatly simplifies calculations on tables of figures, as required in accounting or managing a household budget, for example. The spreadsheet initially consists of a large blank grid made up of rows and columns. Data consisting mainly of numbers but also text is entered into the blank *cells* or rectangles at the junction of each row and column. First the data is entered by typing into the cells, followed by selection from a menu of the appropriate mathematical functions such as totalling rows or columns.

	File	Edit	View	Insert	Format	Tools	Window	Help	

	Arial		10			B	I	U	Σ

	C16						

	A	B	C	D	E	F	G
1							
2			Weekly Spending				
3							
4		Week 1	Week 2	Week 3	Week 4	Total	Average
5							
6	Food	42.65	37.97	46.41	48.57	175.60	43.90
7	Heating	19.28	21.42	23.42	21.48	85.60	21.40
8	Electricity	9.47	11.97	10.97	12.01	44.42	11.11

You can also build up your own formulae for more complex calculations. The spreadsheet saves time by its ability to *replicate*. Having been "told" what to do once, it can then repeat the same calculation down a column or along a row of figures, at lightning speed. Thousands of calculations can be carried out in a few seconds, compared with hours or days required by a human being using more traditional methods.

Data from the spreadsheet can be displayed in various graphical formats such as pie charts and histograms.

The Role of the Database

The database is a collection of similar records, where all the records have exactly the same layout.

		Destination	Date	Departs From	Days	Price
✔	1	Canadian Rockies	18/03/2004	Manchester	11	£829
	2	China	18/03/2004	Heathrow	10	£948
	3	Dublin	25/03/2004	East Midlands	3	£145
	4	Eden Project	19/04/2004	(Local Coach)	4	£185
	5	Highland Railways	10/04/2004	N/A	5	£249
	6	Malta	15/03/2004	Birmingham	12	£259

Holidays.wdb - Microsoft Works Database
File Edit View Record Format Tools Help
Arial 10

However, the modern database program is much more than a replacement for the simple card index system. Apart from the ability to *search* for records meeting certain criteria, the records can be automatically *sorted* into a particular order such as date or alphabetical order.

Records may be *edited* to reflect any changes in the data. For example personnel records must be updated when a person moves house or changes jobs. An important feature of the Works database is the ability to generate both *graphs* and *reports*. These enable the results of any information retrieval operations to be presented in a clear and attractive format which is easy to understand.

A database file can be saved on a floppy or hard disc and retrieved and edited at a later date, before printing on paper. Extracts from a database file can be transferred to the Works word processor for inclusion in a document such as a sales report.

Internet Explorer and E-mail

Also included in the Works package are the well-known Internet Explorer Web browser and the Outlook Express e-mail program. If your computer has a modem fitted, Internet Explorer will connect to the Internet and browse the Web pages for information. You can search for the latest information on any subject under the sun, such as health, travel, gardening or researching your family tree. You can even find a weekend break and reserve accommodation at one of the many on-line hotels and guest houses. Or you can make a purchase from one of the on-line stores such as books and CDs from Amazon.

Outlook Express is an e-mail program allowing you to communicate using text messages, with friends, relatives or colleagues anywhere in the world. These can include file *attachments* such as documents produced in other Works programs, like the word processor, spreadsheet or database. You can even send photographs and video clips down the telephone lines as attachments to your e-mails.

Word Processing

Introduction

Word processing is probably the most frequently used computing application in the office and in the home. Many new computer systems are supplied with word processing software already installed on the hard disc, frequently as part of the popular Microsoft Works suite of software.

Some versions of Microsoft Works also include Microsoft Word, the most popular word processing program in the world. This chapter is based on the standard word processor included in Microsoft Works. However, the methods and principles described in this chapter are relevant to all of the popular word processing software, such as Microsoft Word and Lotus WordPro.

Word processing is far more than simply a replacement for the typewriter as a means of entering text. Some of the advantages of the word processor, compared with the typewriter, are as follows:

- Corrections can be made on the screen before printing on paper, so there is no evidence of any alterations. Several copies can easily be printed.

- Documents are saved on disc, then retrieved later. This allows a document to be used again, perhaps with small changes such as a new date. There is no need to retype the whole document.

- Text can be *edited* more easily - whole blocks of text can be inserted, deleted or moved to a new position in the document.

- The *Find and Replace* feature enables a word (or group of words) to be exchanged for another word or words, wherever they occur in a document. For example, replace "house" with "property".

- Text can be formatted with effects such as bold and italic and in various fonts or styles of lettering as shown below.

Brush Script

- The layout of the page can easily be changed, with different margins, line spacing, graphical effects and newspaper-style columns.

- Modern word processors contain many additional features such as spelling and grammar checkers, a thesaurus and a word count facility.

Typical uses for a word processor are:

- Typing letters and reports.
- Producing a document including tables, graphs, and pictures.
- Editing a magazine or newsletter for a club, society or neighbourhood.
- Printing certificates of achievement, etc.

- Preparing a cover sheet or text for a fax or e-mail.
- Addressing envelopes.
- Producing a flyer or leaflet using special text and graphical effects.

- Creating and editing a Curriculum Vitae.
- Typesetting a full size novel or text book (such as this one) or a college dissertation or thesis.

Preparing a Letter

For many people, keeping in touch with family and friends with a well thought out letter is preferable to a hastily drafted e-mail. If you are a setting up a new venture, a well-presented business plan and correspondence is essential if you are to have a professional image.

The next few pages go through the main steps in using the word processor to produce a simple document such as a letter. Initially it is suggested that you read through the text to get a feel for the skills involved. Then you may wish to attempt the exercise at the end of this chapter and complete the skills checklist.

Starting a New Document

The Microsoft Works word processor can be started from the **Task Launcher** by clicking on the **Word Proc...** icon on the Works **Home** screen, shown right and below.

Alternatively, the word processor can be started by clicking **start, All Programs, Microsoft Works** and **Microsoft Works Word Processor**.

You are presented with a blank screen ready to start typing.

A word processor must start with numerous *default settings*, such as the page margins. You may wish to change these later, but for the time being, you can safely accept most of the default values which Works provides.

The default lettering style or *font* (normally **Times New Roman**, size **10** shown above) can easily be changed after clicking the down arrows shown right and on the toolbar below.

A popular font for this type of document is **Arial** size **12**.

Setting the Paper Size

You need to ensure that the paper size in your document on the screen matches the actual paper used by your printer. Select **File, Page Setup...** and **Source, Size & Orientation**. Choose the size of the paper you are using in your printer, usually **A4,** as shown below.

Orientation in the above **Page Setup** dialogue box refers to whether the finished printout should be viewed with the paper in the **Portrait** position (long sides vertical) or **Landscape** (long sides horizontal).

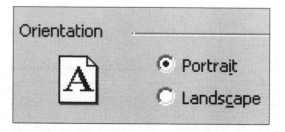

Creating a New File Using Save As...

Before you start entering the actual text of a document it's a good idea to create a file with a suitable name. Then it's a simple matter to quickly save the document at intervals while you are entering the text. Select **File** and **Save As...** and enter a meaningful **File name** such as **Letter to hotel**. File names can be up to 255 characters long.

Save As		? X
Save in: ⌂ My Documents	▼ ⇐ 🗀 📂 ▦▾	

⌂ My Pictures

File name:	Letter to hotel.wps	Save
Save as type:	Works Document (*.wps) ▼	Cancel
		Template...

Creating a New Folder

Note that by default the document will be saved as a file in the folder **My Documents**, unless you have selected another folder. You can create a new folder within the folder **My Documents** after clicking on the icon shown on the right and also shown in the **Save As** dialogue box above.

A highlighted name, **New Folder** appears, as shown on the next page.

Save As

Save in: 📁 My Documents ▼

📁 My eBooks
📁 My Music
📁 My Pictures
📁 New Folder

Replace the words **New Folder**, by typing in your own name for the folder, such as **Holidays**. Saving and organizing your work into folders which you have created is covered later in this book.

Regular Saving - the Quick Save

Suppose you work for a long session, say 2 or more hours, and don't bother to save your work. A sudden power cut or computer "glitch" could cause all that effort to be wasted. Regular saving every few minutes is quick and easy and can prevent this unnecessary frustration.

After the initial **Save As...**, when you give the file a name, all subsequent saves can be achieved by simply clicking the disc icon on the toolbar shown right and below.

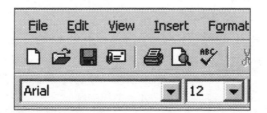

Entering the Text

Shown below is a short sample letter. In the exercise at the end of this chapter you will be asked to enter this letter or make up a similar one of your own.

Dove Cottage

Rudyard

Staffordshire

SB5 NJ6

5 January 2003

The Manager

The Milton International Hotel

Ontario

Canada

Dear Sir/Madam

I am planning to attend a family reunion in Ontario in June of this year and your hotel has been recommended by one of my relatives.

I would be most grateful if you could send me a copy of your latest brochure, including details of your facilities for the disabled and car hire.

Yours faithfully

John Williamson

Hints for Absolute Beginners:

- You don't need to press the **Enter** or **Return** key at the end of a line. Just keep typing and the word processor takes care of everything in a process known as word wrap.

- You only need to press **Enter** or **Return** at the end of a line if you want to start a new paragraph or insert one or more blank lines.

- Use the **Tab** key (shown on the right) to jump across to a fixed point on a line - e.g. to vertically align the left-hand edges of the lines of an address.

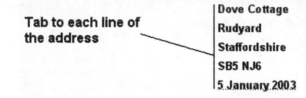

Tab to each line of the address

Dove Cottage
Rudyard
Staffordshire
SB5 NJ6
5 January 2003

Correcting Mistakes While Typing

While you're entering the text, correct any typing errors by deleting the mistake then typing the correct text. Words to the *left* of the cursor are deleted with the backspace key (shown left), while the **Delete** key removes text to the *right* of the cursor. Periodically, while you are entering text, click the floppy disc icon on the toolbar to carry out a quick save. Printing can sometimes result in a computer "crashing" or locking up, causing the current document in the memory to be lost. So it's best to save your work before attempting to make a printout on paper.

Setting Your Own Tab Stops

When you need to start several lines of text a long way from the left margin, the **Tab** key is used to make sure that successive lines all start in exactly the same place. For example, ensuring the lines of an address are vertically aligned on the left. Beginners often use the space bar to move across the screen to the point where text is to start. Unfortunately, using this method, the alignment is often lost when the document is printed on paper. Using the **Tab** key however, the cursor jumps across to exactly the same position on every line on the screen and the alignment is maintained on the printout on paper.

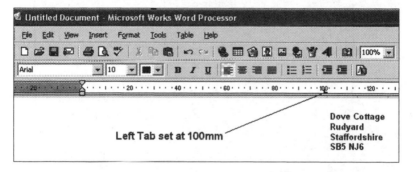

In the screenshot above a *Left Tab* has been set at 100mm, as discussed shortly. (As described shortly, you can change the units to inches or centimetres if you prefer).

Word processors normally have several default **Tab** stops already set. However, it's useful to be able to set your own using the **Tabs** dialogue box shown below and accessed from **Format** and **Tabs**....

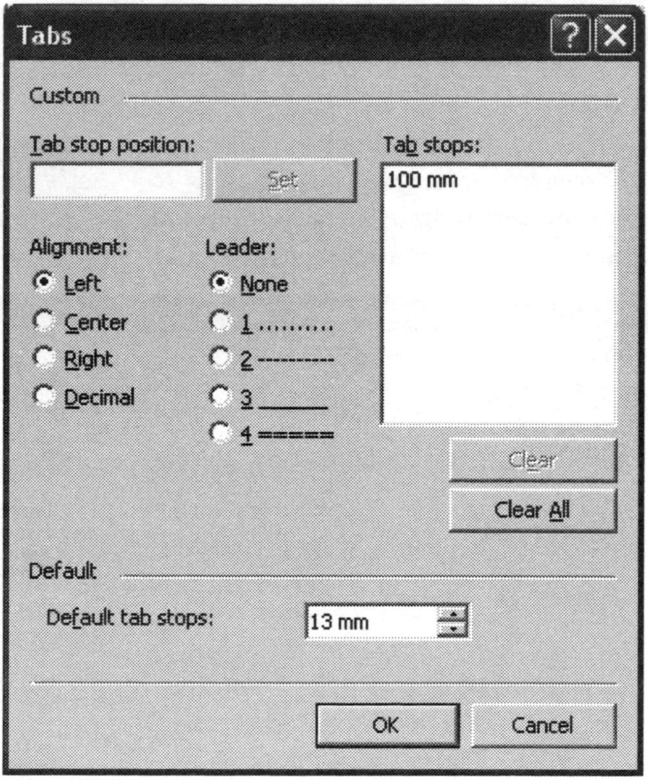

Enter the required measurement in **Tab stop position:** and click **Set** and **OK**.

If you prefer to work in inches or centimetres, select **Tools**, **Options...** and **Measurement units:** and click the down arrow to change the units using the drop-down menu.

Options
General
Measurement units: Centimeters ▼
Inches
Centimeters
Millimeters
Proofing Tools   Points
Picas

Having set a **Tab** stop, press the **Tab** key to move to the required starting position in the document. Notice in the

Alignment:
- ⦿ Left
- ○ Center
- ○ Right
- ○ Decimal

Tabs dialogue box on the previous page, there are four different types of **Tab** stop, allowing you to align the text on the **Right**, **Left** or about the **Center**. The **Decimal Tab** causes columns of numbers to be vertically aligned about the decimal point.

Leaders

Referring to the **Tabs** dialogue box on the previous page, the radio buttons under the word **Leader** enable the **Tab** position to be preceded by a choice of dotted or continuous lines. This idea is often used in the contents page of a book, for example.

Leader:
- ⦿ None
- ○ 1 ....
- ○ 2 ----------
- ○ 3 _____
- ○ 4 =====

Chapter 7 85

Leader

Creating a Template for Your Own Headed Paper

To save typing in your address at the top of every letter you write, you could make a template for headed paper containing your address and any other information. Start a new document and use the **Tab** key to set up your name and address. Then select **File** and **Save As...** and click the **Template...** button. Save the template with a name such as **my address**. Whenever you want to start a new letter, from the Works **Task Launcher**, select **Tasks** and **Personal Templates**.

Select the template, in this case called **my address**, and click **Start this task** to launch the new document with the address already in place, ready for you to begin typing.

Print Preview

Before you make a printout on paper, you might wish to select **Print Preview** to give a screen view of how the document will print on paper. Click **File** and **Print Preview** from the word processor menu bar. Alternatively, use the **Preview** button on the main **Print** dialogue box accessed via **File** and **Print....** Or click the **Print Preview** icon on the word processor toolbar.

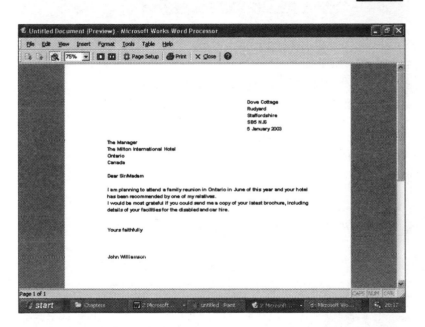

The **Print Preview** allows you to check the layout of your document before it is printed on paper. You may, for example, decide to insert a few blank lines here and there just to make the document more readable. When you are finished with the **Preview** click **Close** to return to the main word processor window.

Printing on Paper

Use **File** and **Print...** then click **OK** to make a copy of your letter on paper. Notice that there are options to specify the number of copies and the particular page(s) to be printed, in the case of longer documents.

Print		? ✕
Printer		
Name:	HP LaserJet 5L (PCL) ▼	Properties
Status:	Ready	
Type:	HP LaserJet 5L (PCL)	
Where:	LPT1:	
Comment:		☐ Print to file

Print Range	Copies
⦿ All	Number of copies: 1 ▲▼
◯ Pages from: 1 to: 1	☑ Collate

Mail Merge Print Settings

☐ Don't print lines with empty fields
☐ Send merge result to a new document

Print a sample of your document

[Test]

[Preview]   [OK]   [Cancel]

Alternatively, if you just want a quick print using the existing **Print** dialogue box settings, click the **Print** icon on the word processor toolbar.

Practice Exercise

You may wish to copy the letter on page 135 or alternatively make up a letter of your own. To complete the whole of this exercise you need to have a printer attached to your computer. Although the exercise is based on the Microsoft Works word processor, the basic operations are similar for word processors in general.

1 Start up your word processing program and open a blank document.

2 Set the text font, e.g. **Arial 12**.

3 Set the paper size to match the paper in your printer, e.g. **A4**.

4 Create a new file, e.g. **Holidays 2004**.

5 Set a **Tab** stop ready for the address on the letter.

6 Enter the text for the letter.

7 Practise using the **Delete** key and backspace keys to delete or correct words as you are typing. Also practise inserting words.

8 Save the work at regular intervals and also after you have finished entering text.

9 Check the layout using **Print Preview**.

10 Make any necessary adjustments, e.g. increase the spacing by inserting blank lines using the **Enter** key.

11 Make a printout on paper.

Keyboard Shortcuts

Save: **Ctrl+S**

Print: **Ctrl+P**

Checklist: Basic Word Processing

If you have successfully completed the previous exercise you should now be able to use a word processor to produce a basic text document, such as a letter. You may wish to use the following list to tick off the skills you have already acquired and possibly revisit any which need more time.

Word Processing Skills	Achieved
Start a new word processing document.	
Set the text *font*, i.e. the style and size of lettering.	
Set the paper size to match the paper in your printer.	
Create a new file with a meaningful file name.	
Set a Tab Stop using suitable units of measurement	
Use the Tab key to vertically align text.	
Enter text using upper and lower case letters.	
Correct errors as they occur during the entry of text.	
Save a document at regular intervals.	
Use the Print Preview feature.	
Print a document on paper.	

The next chapter covers more advanced topics such as altering the content and appearance of a document.

Editing a Document

Introduction

One of the best things about the word processor is the fact that if you don't like the content or appearance of a document you can easily change it. You can take a document saved on your hard disc, open it in your word processor and carve it about as much as you like. There's none of the mess associated with old fashioned "cutting and pasting" with scissors and glue. Then when you have finished editing you simply print out the revised version incorporating all of the changes. In fact, "cutting and pasting" is still used to describe moving a piece of text within a document or between documents. This is done using the cutting, copying and pasting icons from your word processor toolbar as shown on the right and below. This topic is described in detail later in this chapter.

Untitled Document - Microsoft Works Word Processor

File Edit View Insert Format Tools Table Help

Times New Roman   10   B I U

Retrieving a Document from the Hard Disc

Having created a document and saved it on disc you can retrieve it at any time. From the menu bar select **File** and **Open**. As discussed in the previous chapter, a letter was saved with the name **Holidays 2004**. It was saved in the folder **Holidays**, which was created in the folder **My Documents**. You may need to click the down arrow to the right of the **Look in:** bar, shown below, to select the required folder on your **C:** drive (hard disc). If necessary please see the previous chapter, for more information on files and folders.

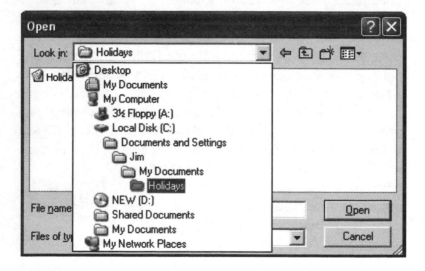

When you have located the required folder containing your file, click on the filename so that it appears in the **File name:** slot, as shown on the next page.

Now click **Open** for the document to be opened up in your word processor.

Then you might wish to proof read the document and improve it using editing operations as follows:

- Deleting text.
- Replacing text.
- Moving blocks of text.
- Inserting words or blocks of text.
- Correcting spelling mistakes.
- Adding text to extend a document.

Undoing Actions

When editing a document it's easy to make a mistake like deleting the wrong words. Fortunately the **Undo** feature accessed off the **Edit** menu shown below allows you to reverse *the last action*. Or you can use the **Undo** icon off the word processor toolbar, shown right and below.

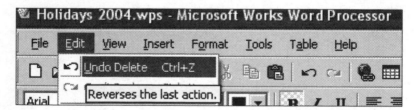

Please note that the **Undo** feature can be used to reverse a variety of editing tasks, not just deleting text as in this example. Please also note that if you prefer you can use the keyboard alternative **Ctrl+Z**, which means "Hold down the **Ctrl** key and press **Z**".

Block Operations on Selected Text

A lot of small editing tasks can be achieved by simply moving the cursor to the appropriate place and deleting or inserting text. However, you may wish to delete or move entire lines, paragraphs or even pages of text. For these tasks you first *select* the text, so that it's *highlighted* against a black background.

The Polytunnel

The polytunnel is similar to a greenhouse but considerably cheaper. It consists of a steel tubular frame over which is stretched a sheet of polythene.

The main use of the polytunnel is to grow plants and shrubs and many polytunnels are now in use with both private and commercial growers. The polytunnel, despite some early reservations, has proved to be durable and able to withstand the worst of Britain's weather.

Apart from its use in horticulture, the polytunnel can be found in a variety of situations. Some polytunnels are used to provide shelter for farm animals such as sheep, while others provide a sheltered work space or storage area. Others are used as covers for outdoor swimming pools.

Selecting Text Using the Mouse

- To select any piece of text, keep the left mouse button held down while moving the pointer across the whole of the required text.

- To select an individual word double-click over the word.

- To select a line of text, make a single click in the left margin of the document.

- To select a paragraph, double-click in the left margin.

- To select the whole document, treble-click in the left margin or use **Edit** and **Select All** off the menus.

Selecting Text Using the Keyboard

In general, each of the Works menu options has a keyboard alternative as shown on the right. So you can also select the whole document using **Ctrl+A**. This means, while holding down the **Ctrl** (Control) key, press the letter **A**. Another method is to place the cursor at the beginning of the required block of text then, while holding down the **Shift** key, shown

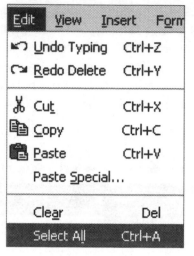

left, use the arrow keys, shown below, to select the block of text.

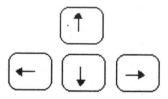

Deleting a Block of Text

Select the required text and press the **Delete** key. (Or place the cursor on the left of the required text and hold down the **Delete** key.)

Inserting Text

Insert text by placing the cursor where the new text is to begin then start typing. The new text should force its way in without deleting any of the old text. If the new text *over-types* and replaces the existing text rather than pushing its way in, press the **Insert** key to switch off over-type mode.

```
Insert
```

Search and Replace

To replace a word or group of words wherever they occur in a document, select **Edit** and **Replace...** to open up the **Find and Replace** dialogue box. For example, to replace the word "business" with "company" throughout a document. Enter the old word in **Find what:** and enter the new word in **Replace with:** as shown in the next dialogue box.

Now click the **Replace All** button to replace the old word(s) with the new word (s) throughout the document. Notice in the above dialogue box there are options to match the case (i.e. capital or small letters, also known as upper and lower case) and also to match only whole words.

Moving a Block of Text - Cut and Paste

Select the block of text to be moved as shown below.

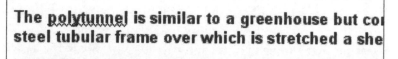

The **polytunnel** is similar to a greenhouse but co
steel tubular frame over which is stretched a she

The main use of the polytunnel is to grow plants
now in use with both private and commercial gro
early reservations, has proved to be durable and
Britain's weather.

Now click the scissors icon on the Works toolbar.   This removes the selected text and stores it on the "clipboard". The clipboard is a temporary storage location where text (and graphics) can be held until you are ready to place them somewhere else in the document.

Next move the cursor to wherever you want the selected text to start. Now click the paste icon on the toolbar (shown left) to place the text in its new position.

Cutting and pasting can also be achieved using the **Edit** menu after you have selected the text.

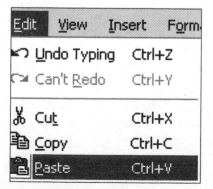

If you want to *duplicate* a piece of text rather then *move* it, then use the copy icon off the menu bar shown right or the **Copy** command off the **Edit** menu shown on the previous page.

Cut and Paste using the clipboard is a very useful skill in a variety of Windows applications, not just for moving text within a document. For example you can move a graphic by copying it from a paint program to the clipboard and then pasting it into a word processing document. You can also use cut and paste to move files between your folders in the Windows Explorer.

Checking Spelling

The spelling checker invoked from **Tools** and **Spelling and Grammar...** suggests alternative spellings, improvements in grammar and spacing between words.

Spelling and Grammar: English (United Kingdom)   [?] [X]

Not in dictionary:

suport

Ignore Once
Ignore All
Add

Suggestions:

support
sport

Change
Change All

Spelling options

☑ Ignore words in UPPERCASE
☑ Ignore words with numbers
☑ Ignore Internet and file addresses
☐ Check grammar

Options...

Close

Formatting a Document

After you have checked the content and spelling, you may want to change the appearance of a document. This is known as *formatting* and includes different fonts or styles and sizes of lettering and text effects such as bold, italics and underlining. Formatting also includes page layout features such as the margins between the text and the edges of the page, alterations to the space between lines of text and various ways of aligning the vertical edges of the text.

If you know the formatting you want to use, it can be set before you begin typing. For example, you could switch italics on before typing a particular word then switch it off again. Alternatively, you can enter the text of your document without any effects and then apply the formatting afterwards.

The Formatting Toolbar

On the left of the toolbar above is the font name and size, changed by clicking the down arrows and selecting from the drop-down menus. The next drop-down menu, obtained by clicking the down arrow shown on the right, allows you to change the text colour.

Next are the three main text effects bold, italic and underline. These effects can also be switched on by holding down the **Ctrl** key and pressing either **B**, **I** or **U**. Effects like these operate as "toggles" - you use the same method to switch them on as to switch them off.

The icons on the right of the formatting toolbar represent different methods of text alignment.

Reading from left to right, the actions of the 4 icons on the right and their alternative keyboard shortcuts are:

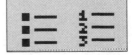

- Aligned left edge, ragged right.   **Ctrl+L**

- Aligned to the centre.   **Ctrl+E**

- Aligned right, ragged left.   **Ctrl+R**

- Justified text (aligned left and right).   **Ctrl+J**

- Remove any of the above.   **Ctrl+Q**

The problem with fully justified text is that in order to achieve the vertical alignment on the right-hand edge, the text may be filled with too many spaces between words producing unsightly "rivers of white".

The next two tools on the right of the formatting toolbar allow lists to be highlighted with either bullets or numbers.

The last two formatting tools shown are used to decrease or increase the indent at the start of a paragraph.

Applying Formatting Effects:

1 Select (or highlight) the required block of text.

2 Apply the formatting by clicking the appropriate icon on the toolbar, or selecting the relevant menu command or using the equivalent keyboard shortcut.

3 When the formatting has taken effect, remove the highlighting by clicking outside of the selected area.

Changing Line Spacing

Sometimes you may want to set a paragraph or indeed a whole document with extra spacing between lines. Double spacing, for example, is often used on draft documents to allow extra space for comments and suggestions to be added by hand. Line spacing can be adjusted after clicking the **Spacing** tab in the **Format Paragraph** dialogue box shown previously. **Lines Before:** and **Lines After:** allow you to adjust the space above and below a paragraph.

Changing the Page Margins

The margins around the text are set by default at 2.54cm (or 1 inch) for the top and bottom and 3.17cm for the left and right. (Please see the note on page 139 if you prefer to work in inches). You might want to increase the size of the margins to allow comments to be written on a draft document or decrease them to allow more text to fit on a page. To change the margins select **File, Page Setup...** and the **Margins** tab.

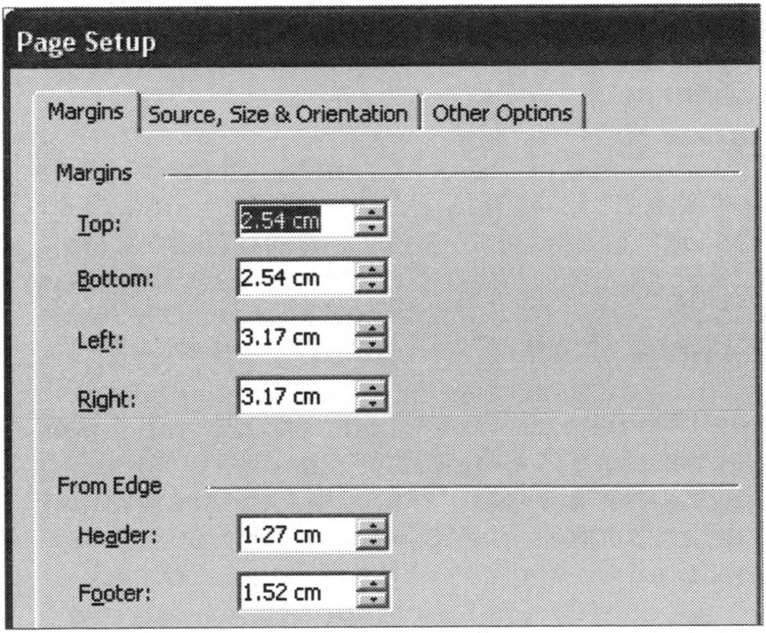

Page Setup

| Margins | Source, Size & Orientation | Other Options |

Margins

Top: 2.54 cm

Bottom: 2.54 cm

Left: 3.17 cm

Right: 3.17 cm

From Edge

Header: 1.27 cm

Footer: 1.52 cm

Header: and **Footer:** shown above refer to text which you can place in the top and bottom margins, as discussed later in this chapter. For example, in this book the title of each chapter is placed in the header and the page number is placed in the footer.

Practice Exercise - Word Processing

In order to practise the skills covered in this chapter, you may wish to copy the following text into your word processor. Then apply the editing and formatting skills given in the exercise. Alternatively make up a short document of your own, consisting of a few paragraphs.

The Polytunnel

The polytunnel is similar to a greenhouse but considerably cheaper. It consists of a steel tubular frame over which is stretched a sheet of polythene.

The main use of the polytunnel is to grow plants and shrubs and many polytunnels are now in use with both private and commercial growers. The polytunnel, despite some early reservations, has proved to be durable and able to withstand the worst of Britain's weather.

Apart from its use in horticulture, the polytunnel can be found in a variety of situations. Some polytunnels are used to provide shelter for farm animals such as sheep, while others provide a sheltered work space or storage area. Others are used as covers for outdoor swimming pools.

The practice exercise is given on the next page.

1. Open up your word processor program and copy the notes on the polytunnel on the previous page. Centre the title using the centring icon. Change the font and apply bold and italics.

2. Save the text as a file with a suitable filename in the folder **My Documents** or in a folder of your choice.

3. For practice close the file down by clicking the **X** in the top right-hand corner. Then practise retrieving the file using **File** and **Open** from the menu bar.

4. Select the whole document and set it to fully justified text.

5. Select the last sentence and delete it. Practise the **Undo** feature by reversing a delete action.

6. Make up a new paragraph and insert it after the first paragraph. Set the new paragraph in double-line spacing.

7. Select the paragraph starting **The main use of...** and use "cut and paste" so that it becomes the last.

8. Use the indent tool on the formatting toolbar to indent the second paragraph.

9. Use **Edit** and **Replace** to change the word **polytunnel** to **poly-tunnel** throughout the document.

10. Make a deliberate spelling mistake and correct it using the spelling checker.

11. Change the margins on your document.

12. Save the document on your hard disc and make a printout on paper.

Checklist: Editing a Document

If you have worked through the practical exercise in this chapter you will have covered a lot of essential skills for editing documents in a word processor. You may wish to use the following list to tick those skills you have successfully accomplished and perhaps have another attempt at any which need more practice.

Word Processing Skills	Achieved
Retrieve a previously saved file from disc.	
Select, i.e. highlight, words, paragraphs, documents.	
Change the appearance of text using different fonts and effects such as bold and italic.	
Delete and insert words and blocks of text.	
Replace words throughout an entire document.	
Use "cut and paste" to move text within a document.	
Use the spelling checker to find and correct mistakes.	
Format a paragraph using justification and indentation.	
Change the spacing between lines.	
Change the page margins.	
Use the undo feature to reverse an action.	

Further Word Processing Skills

The next few pages cover some miscellaneous word processing skills which can be used to enhance a document.

Inserting a Table

The word processor has a table feature which is easy to use. From the **Table** menu on the word processor menu bar, select **Insert Table....** The following dialogue box appears:

Insert Table				? ☒
Select a format:		Number of rows:	2	
(None)		Number of columns:	2	
Basic Table				
Simple: Box		Row height:	Auto	
Simple: Column				
Simple: Band		Column width:	Auto	
Simple: Ledger				

Example:

Sales	Buyer	Model	Color	Paid
Mon	MS	JK4	Red	Cash
Tues	WT	AISG1	Blue	Credit
Wed	KK	SSDS9	White	Credit
Thurs	DH	RMDM	Blue	Credit

OK   Cancel

Several styles of table are available under **Select a format:** and you can specify the number of rows and columns. The **Row height:** and **Column width:** are specified at this stage or they can be adjusted later by dragging with the mouse.

When you have selected the format and number of rows and columns, etc., click **OK** to insert the table in your document. The cursor appears in the top left-hand cell, ready for you to start entering the data into the table.

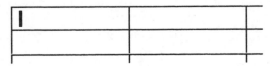

The cells in a table can be selected and edited using the drop-down **Table** menu shown below.

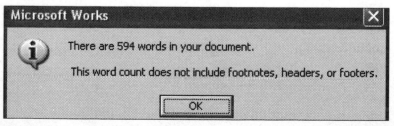

In the **Table** menu shown above, when you choose to **Select** an object such as a cell or row, etc., the selected object is highlighted on the screen. Then the contents of the selected cell(s) can be formatted or deleted, as required.

Word Count

Sometimes a document is limited to a prescribed number of words - as in the case of an article for publication in a magazine. Select **Tools** and **Word Count** to find how many words have been written.

Using Columns

Text can be set in two or more newspaper style columns, by clicking **Format** and **Columns...** on the word processor menu bar. The columns can be set before typing the text or after selecting an existing piece of text by dragging over it with the mouse. In the Works word processor the columns apply to the whole document and can include a dividing line in the adjustable space between columns.

In the Microsoft Word word processor, if you choose to work in two or more columns, you can choose to apply the columns to the whole document or **This point forward**. So, for example, you could have a title or opening paragraph all the way across the page followed by text in two columns.

Headers and Footers

These are used in longer documents and allow a title and information such as the page number, document name or date to be added along the top or bottom of every page.

For example, on the pages of this book, the chapter title, e.g. 10   Editing a Document, has been set up as a header. The page number has been set up as a footer.

From the word processor menu bar, select **View** and **Header and Footer**. Empty boxes for the header and footer appear on the page.

```
Header
  3 Garden Design
```

You can type your own text freely into the header and footer boxes, as shown above. Or you can use the header and footer toolbar, shown below, which appears automatically on the screen, after you click **View** and **Header and Footer**. This allows you to insert information in the header and footer on every page, such as the page number or current date.

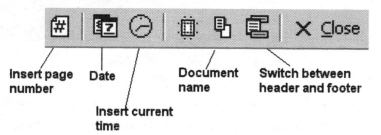

Insert page number   Date   Insert current time   Document name   Switch between header and footer

After you have selected the required information from the icons on the toolbar shown above, click **Close**. The selected information will now appear in the headers and footers on every page, suitably incremented where necessary.

Keyboard Shortcuts

You may prefer to use the following keyboard shortcuts as an alternative to mouse operations. For example, to switch bold lettering on (and off), use **Ctrl+B**. This means "While holding down the **Ctrl** key, press the **B** key."

Ctrl+C	Copy text
Ctrl+X	Cut text
Ctrl+V	Paste text
Ctrl+Z	Undo previous action
Ctrl+A	Select entire document
Ctrl+B	Switch bold text on and off
Ctrl+U	Switch underline on and off
Ctrl+I	Switch Italic text on and off
Ctrl+E	Centre paragraph
Ctrl+J	Justify paragraph
Ctrl+L	Align paragraph left
Ctrl+R	Align paragraph right
Ctrl+Q	Remove paragraph formatting
Ctrl+1	Single-spaced text
Ctrl+5	1½ spaced text
Ctrl+2	Double-spaced text
Ctrl+N	Open new (blank) document
Ctrl+O	Open existing document
Ctrl+S	Save document
Ctrl+P	Print document

In general, the above keyboard shortcuts are applied after first selecting the block of text. As described earlier, text is selected with the mouse or by holding down the shift key and traversing the text with one of the arrow keys. Effects such as Bold, Italic and Underline can be switched on before the text is typed.

10 Editing a Document

Desktop Publishing

Introduction

Desktop publishing involves the use of various software tools to change the appearance and layout of text. Originally, word processors were used for the creation of documents using only plain text, similar to the output from an ordinary typewriter. Documents using more elaborate effects such as graphics and different styles of text required special desktop publishing software. Modern word processors however, now contain many desktop publishing features, so that quite impressive documents can be created. This book, for example, was typeset entirely in Microsoft Word 2002, which is very similar to the word processor in Microsoft Works.

The desktop publishing features covered in this section are:

- Text in different sizes and styles of letters or *fonts*.
- Borders and background shading.
- Pictures inserted into the text in documents.
- Bullets and numbering to highlight lists.
- Microsoft WordArt, a feature used to manipulate text into various shapes.

Care has to be taken with the use of fonts. It's easy to spoil a serious document with the over-zealous use of fancy lettering. The more exotic fonts are best kept for more light-hearted publications such as greeting cards, flyers and invitations.

Fonts

When Microsoft Windows is first set up on a computer, a large number of fonts are installed as part of the process. Many of these are known as TrueType fonts and are *scalable*. This means the lettering can be enlarged or reduced without departing from the original design.

A font is a particular design or style of lettering in a particular size. The size is measured in units called *points* where 72 points are equal to one inch. So if you wanted to print a title, say, in letters ½ an inch high, you would set a font size of 36 points. This is shown in the example below, which uses the Times New Roman font.

Milton Orchid Club

The fonts used by Microsoft Works are part of the Windows operating system. To examine the list of installed fonts, click the down-arrow to the right of the current font on the word processor toolbar - in this case Times New Roman. Below is just a small sample of the available fonts - scrolling down the list reveals many more.

Although your computer probably contains far more fonts than you'll ever need, you can add even more using the **Fonts** folder in the **Control Panel** - accessed from the **start** menu. In fact, if you look at any professional publication you'll find that very few different font designs are used - frequently only one or two per document. Books and newspapers frequently use the Times New Roman and Arial fonts, as used in this paragraph

A choice of font sizes appears when you click the down-arrow to the right of the current font size on the word processor toolbar.

Further options for changing the fonts and applying different effects are available in the **Font** dialogue box accessed from **Format** and **Font...** on the word processor menu bar.

You can see that in addition to changing the font name and size you can use several other text effects. For example, the **Subscript** effect could be used for the $_2$ in H_2O. These effects can be switched on before you begin typing text. Alternatively they can be applied to existing text by selecting the text and then switching on the effect.

Borders and Shading

To emphasise a piece of text, you can enclose it within a border and set the text against a background. A simple method is to insert a **Text Box** using **Insert** and **Text Box** off the word processor menu bar. An empty box appears which you can drag to the desired size and shape, before entering the text.

Then you can choose the border and shading from the dialogue box shown below, obtained by selecting **Format** and **Borders and Shading**....

Choose the border and shading from the drop-down lists under **Border Art:**, **Fill Style:** and **Color 1:**.

> Border Art:
>
> [❀ ❀ ❀ ❀ ❀ ❀] ▼
>
> Border Art Width:
>
> [16 pt] ▲▼
>
> Shading
>
> Fill Style:
>
> [　　　　　] ▼
>
> Color 1:
>
> [☐ Gray - 10%] ▼
>
> Color 2:
>
> [☐ White] ▼

You can also apply a border to a highlighted paragraph or to the whole page. From the word processor menu select **Format** and **Borders and Shading....** The **Apply to:** menu at the top of the **Borders and Shading** dialogue box allows you to place the border around the whole **Page** or just around the **Paragraph**.

> **Borders and Shading**
>
> Apply to:
>
> [Paragraph] ▼
>
> Page
> Paragraph
>
> Line Style:
>
> [━━━━━] ▼
>
> Line Color:
>
> [■ Automatic] ▼

Inserting Pictures

Microsoft Works (and many other programs) include a library of pictures known as *clip art*. These can be inserted into a document to illustrate the text.

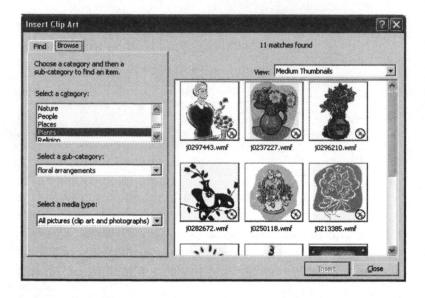

When you insert a picture onto the page of the word processor, the picture is *embedded* so that it becomes an integral part of the page. Apart from clip art, pictures may be inserted from several other sources such as the scanned pictures and photographs saved as files on your hard disc.

 Enter the clip art library by clicking the **Insert Clip Art** icon on the word processor toolbar. Alternatively you can insert pictures (also known as *objects*) from various sources by selecting **Insert** and **Picture** from the menu bar.

Apart from the **Clip Art** option, you can insert pictures **From File...**, i.e. pictures and photographs which have been saved in folders on your hard disc.

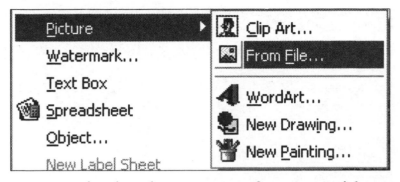

WordArt... in the above menu refers to special text manipulation effects and these are discussed later in this chapter.

New Drawing... and **New Painting...** in the above menu allow you to create your own pictures from scratch using the drawing and painting tools provided in Works and Microsoft Windows.

Having selected the picture you want from whatever source, and clicked **Insert**, the picture is embedded on the page. The picture can then be enlarged or made smaller using grab handles around the frame. The picture can be moved by selecting it then dragging with the mouse. However, for more precise movement of the picture you need to specify the way the text flows around it.

This is known as *wrapping* and is set using **Format** and **Object...** from the menu bar. The **Format Object** dialogue box is shown below.

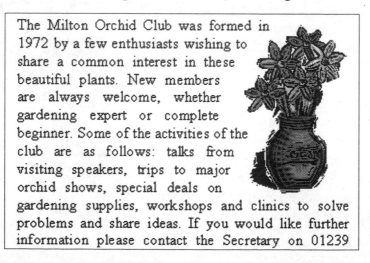

The picture of the flowers below was selected from the **Plants** section of the Works Clip Art. Then the wrapping was set to **Tight** using the **Format Object** dialogue box.

The Milton Orchid Club was formed in 1972 by a few enthusiasts wishing to share a common interest in these beautiful plants. New members are always welcome, whether gardening expert or complete beginner. Some of the activities of the club are as follows: talks from visiting speakers, trips to major orchid shows, special deals on gardening supplies, workshops and clinics to solve problems and share ideas. If you would like further information please contact the Secretary on 01239

Bullets and Numbering

These effects are used to highlight items in a list. A similar method can also be used for applying numbers to a list. Suppose you wanted to highlight the key points in attracting new members to the orchid club:

- Talks by visiting experts

- Trips to major orchid shows

- Special discounts on garden supplies

To create a bulleted list, first select the list of items. Then select **Format** and **Bullets and Numbering...** from the word processor menu bar. There is a huge range of bullets to choose from, as shown below. Similarly, if you select the **Numbered** tab, you are presented with several different styles of numbered list. Click **OK** to apply the bullets.

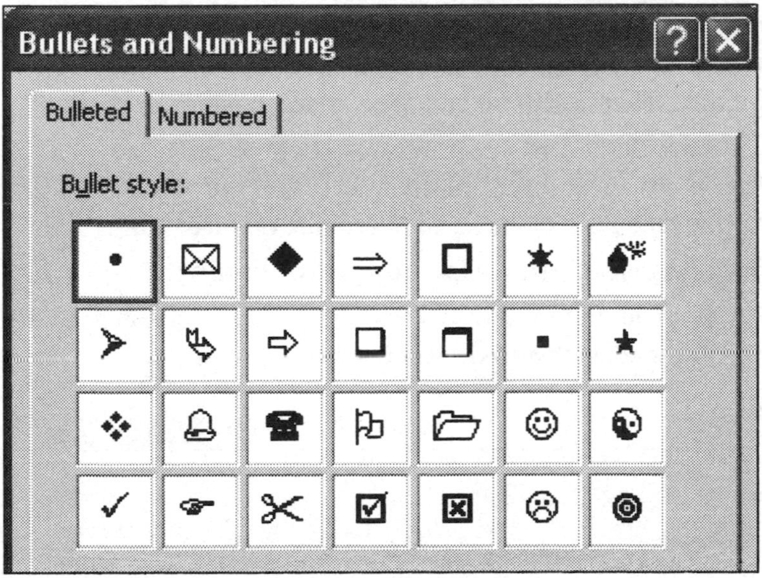

Line Spacing

In order to further highlight the items in the list, you may wish to increase the line spacing (as described earlier in this book). Select the text in the list then from the menu bar click **Format, Paragraph..., Spacing** and choose the spacing required from the drop-down **Line Spacing:** menu. Alternatively use the keyboard shortcuts i.e. select the text then press the **Ctrl** key followed by a number, e.g.:

    Ctrl 5   1½ line spacing

    Ctrl 2   Double line spacing

Microsoft WordArt

This Works feature allows you to manipulate words into different shapes. WordArt is a separate program called up from within the word processor. After you have created the piece of modified text it becomes an *object* which is inserted into the page like a  picture. Then it can be enlarged, made smaller or moved.

To start the WordArt program, click its icon on the word processor toolbar or use the menu options **Insert, Object...**and **Microsoft WordArt 2.0**.

Two things happen when you invoke WordArt:

1. The menu bar across the screen changes to the special WordArt menu, shown below.

— Plain Text ▼	Arial ▼	Best Fit ▼	**B** *I* Ee ◁-A- ᴱ⅋ ᴬᵛ C

2. A small window appears in the word processor page into which you enter the text for your WordArt.

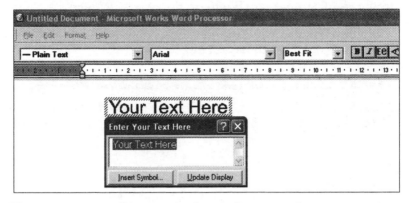

First you enter the required words to replace **Your Text Here**. Then you select the way the text is to be arranged - for example in an arc or slanted. The menu shown below appears after clicking the down-arrow to the right of **Plain Text** in the bar shown above on the left and below.

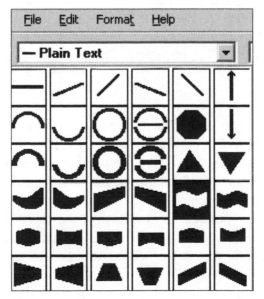

By default the text size is adjusted to fit the WordArt box but you can alter the font size by clicking the down-arrow to the right of **Best Fit** shown on the previous page.

The example below shows the way words can be arranged in a style known as **Deflate (Top)**.

When you click the cross in the corner of the WordArt window, you are returned to the word processor with the WordArt object embedded in the page. Then the WordArt object can be resized like any other graphical object. However, before you can move the WordArt object freely and precisely around the screen you need to set the wrapping to **Square** or **Tight** in **Format, Object...** and **Wrapping**. If you want to edit the WordArt object, double-clicking inside the frame will return you to the WordArt program.

There are many other effects available in WordArt, (in addition to **Bold** and **Italic**) such as the ability to rotate text and to add shading and shadow effects. These are selected from the icons on the right of the WordArt menu bar.

You may wish to experiment with the effect of these icons after placing a piece of text in the WordArt window.

The skills covered in this chapter can be practised by designing a flyer to recruit members to the orchid club.

Practice Exercise

You may wish to copy the flyer on the previous page or make up a flyer or leaflet of your own.

1   Enter the title in its own text box using **Insert** and **Text Box**.

2   Choose a suitable font - **Times New Roman** size **28** is used in this example.

3   Complete the title box with a border and background shading (**Format** and **Borders and Shading....**).

4   Type the body text into the word processor page. Select the body text and experiment with different choices from **Format** and **Bullets and Numbering....**

5   Select the list of features (starting "Talks from visiting...") and experiment with different line spacings. (**Format, Paragraph..., Spacing**).

6   Insert a picture from the clip art library (**Insert, Picture, Clip Art...**) or click the clip art icon. Once on the page, resize the picture as necessary and move it to its final position.

7   The curved lettering "Gardening for All" is produced using the WordArt feature described earlier.

8   Place a border round the whole page using **Format, Borders and Shading...** and **Apply to: Page**.

9   Preview the layout and spacing using **File** and **Print Preview** and make any necessary alterations.

10   Save the document on your hard disc and make a printout on paper.

If you have completed the above exercise you should now be able to practise the skills on some flyers and posters of your own design. Have a look at some good quality professional documents to get ideas for layout and design and the sensible use of fonts.

Checklist: Desktop Publishing

If you have worked through this chapter and completed the practice exercise, you will have acquired many basic desktop publishing skills. You may wish to tick off those skills which you have successfully accomplished and perhaps revise any which need more practice.

Desktop Publishing Skills	Achieved
Change the fonts, i.e. different sizes and styles of letters.	
Create, resize and move a text box.	
Apply background shading to text.	
Apply a border to a text box and to a page.	
Emphasize a list with bullets and extra line spacing.	
Insert a picture or clip art, into a document.	
Alter the "wrapping" or flow of text around a picture.	
Resize a picture and move it around the page.	
Use WordArt to manipulate text into different shapes and apply effects.	

11 Desktop Publishing

Using a Spreadsheet

Introduction

The spreadsheet program is used when *calculations* are needed in tables of figures. A spreadsheet program enables huge tables of figures to be easily displayed, calculated, sorted, printed and presented as graphs and charts.

For anyone who doesn't like mathematics, the spreadsheet is a blessing. This is because the program takes care of all the calculations - you simply tell it what you want to do. The spreadsheet program in Microsoft Works makes this especially simple with a feature called **Easy Calc,** which allows you to select from a menu the calculation you want to perform on a set of figures, as shown below.

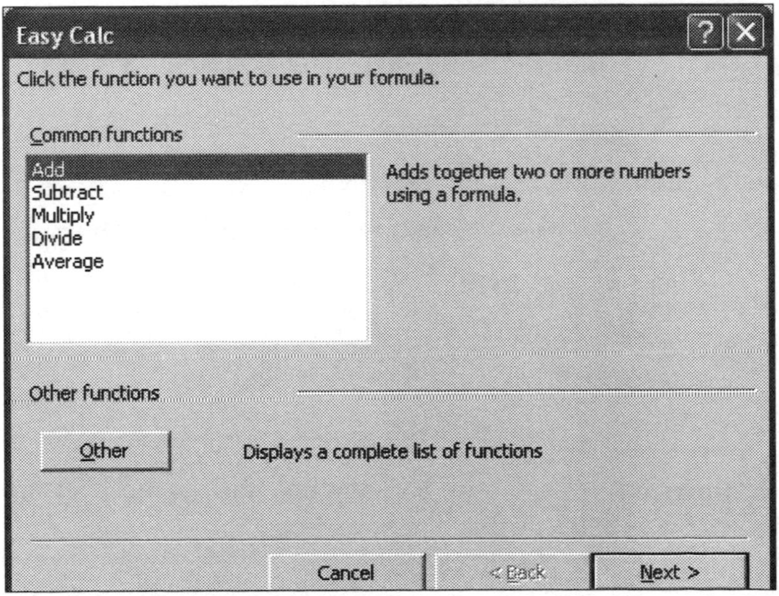

Although the spreadsheet examples in this chapter are based on the Microsoft Works spreadsheet program, working through this chapter will give you the basic skills that are relevant to spreadsheets in general. Indeed, the spreadsheet in Works is very similar to its famous relative Microsoft Excel, the leading business spreadsheet program.

Monitoring Household Spending

Most people need to keep a check on their weekly spending, particularly in later life when income is usually greatly reduced. At the time of writing there is much concern about the reduced value of pensions and there are moves by some companies to reduce their support for employees' pensions.

Whatever your income it's a good idea to monitor your spending and the spreadsheet is designed for just this sort of task. Shown below is a spreadsheet based on the spending of an entirely fictitious household.

	A	B	C	D	E	F	G
1							
2			Weekly Spending				
3							
4		Week 1	Week 2	Week 3	Week 4	Total	Average
5							
6	Food	42.65	37.97	46.41	48.57	175.60	43.90
7	Heating	19.28	21.42	23.42	21.48	85.60	21.40
8	Electricity	9.47	11.97	10.97	12.01	44.42	11.11
9	Rent	85.00	85.00	85.00	85.00	340.00	85.00
10	Petrol	17.27	18.43	21.57	20.87	78.14	19.54
11	Car	19.00	17.00	21.49	26.93	84.42	21.11
12	Total	192.67	191.79	208.86	214.86	808.18	202.05

Step-by-step instructions for creating this spreadsheet are given later in this chapter.

Recalculation

The spreadsheet allows you to speculate on the effect of possible changes, such as an increase in the price of food. These changes can be fed into the spreadsheet, which automatically recalculates all of the totals, etc., affected by the change. The *recalculation* feature is one of the main advantages of spreadsheet programs and can save many hours of work compared with traditional methods of calculation using pencil and paper or pocket calculator.

Graphs and Charts

Apart from the ability to perform the whole range of mathematical calculations, data can be presented in the form of pie charts, bar charts and line graphs, etc.

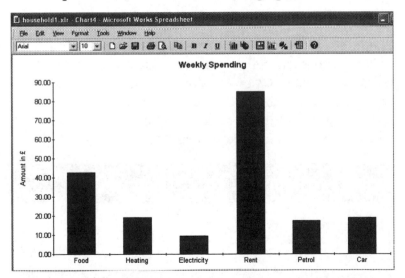

Both the spreadsheet itself and the charts produced from it can be imported into documents in a word processor. This feature is useful, for example, when producing a report on sales performance in a business.

Spreadsheet Basics

The spreadsheet itself is a grid of horizontal rows and vertical columns. Shown below is part of the Microsoft Works spreadsheet, which can extend to a maximum of 16384 rows and 256 columns.

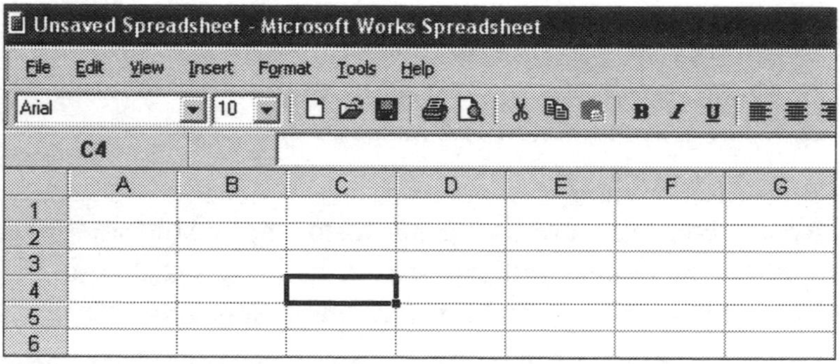

The boxes at the junction of rows and columns are known as *cells* and each cell is uniquely identified by its "grid reference" such as **C4** or **E5**. You can move the cursor from cell to cell using the arrow keys, the **Tab** and **Enter** keys, and the mouse. Or use **Edit** and **Go To...** to move to a cell with a particular reference such as **G23**.

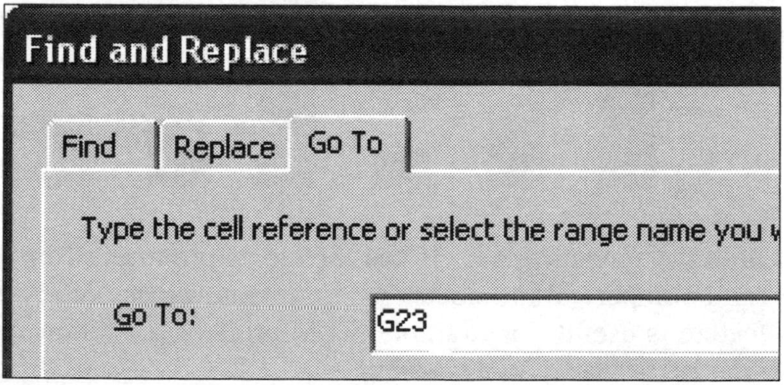

Cell Contents

Various types of data can be entered into a cell:

- *Labels* or text providing headings for rows and columns, e.g. **Food, Heating, Week 1**.

- *Numbers* forming the basic data to be used in calculations.

- *Formulas* to perform calculations like adding up a row or column, e.g. **=SUM(B6:B11)**.

The spreadsheet is a very versatile and forgiving tool; if you make a mistake it's easy to make a correction using the **Delete** key or **Edit** and **Clear** from the menu bar. The spreadsheet itself can be saved as a file on disc and retrieved and printed in a similar way to a word processing document, for example.

Creating a New Spreadsheet

You can start a new spreadsheet by selecting **start, All Programs, Microsoft Works** and **Microsoft Works Spreadsheet**. Alternatively, double-clicking the **Microsoft Works** icon on the Windows Desktop brings up the Works **Task Launcher** shown below. Then select **Works Spreadsheet** and **Start a blank spreadsheet**.

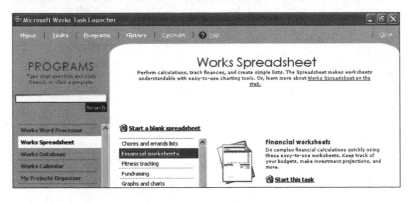

From the **Task Launcher** you can have a look at the list of sample spreadsheets provided. These show what can be achieved with a spreadsheet program and provide quick solutions to specific problems. However, they do not enable you to acquire the skills to create your own spreadsheets from scratch, which are valuable in many situations.

Entering Labels

The example on page 184 uses household spending to demonstrate the creation of a simple spreadsheet. First you would open a blank spreadsheet from the **Task Launcher** or from **start, All Programs, Microsoft Works** and **Microsoft Works Spreadsheet**.

It doesn't matter which cell you start entering the data into - you can always add or delete rows and columns later. Referring to the data on page 184, you would first enter the title **Weekly Spending** and **Week 1, Week 2**, etc., across the top and **Food, Heating**, etc., down the side.

Altering the Size of Columns and Rows

If you need to increase or decrease the width of a column, place the cursor on the vertical line between two column headings, e.g. **A** and **B**. Two 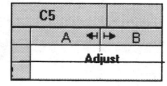 arrows appear which can be dragged to give a column of the required width. The height of rows can be increased or decreased in a similar manner.

Formatting Cells

Common formatting tasks such as bold, italics, centring and justification can be applied by selecting the cell then clicking the appropriate icon on the spreadsheet toolbar, shown right and below.

Alternatively you can apply the entire range of cell formatting effects from the drop-down menu accessed from **Format** and **Font** on the spreadsheet menu bar.

Selecting Rows and Columns

Entire rows or columns can be selected or highlighted by clicking in the cell containing the row or column heading. For example to centre all the **Week** labels click the row header cell (containing the number **4** in this case) to select the row. Then click the centre icon on the toolbar to centre the labels.

	A	B	C	D	E	F	G
1							
2			Weekly Spending				
3							
4			Week 1	Week 2	Week 3	Week 4	Total	Average
5							
6	Food	42.65	37.97	46.41	48.57	175.60	43.90
7	Heating	19.28	21.42	23.42	21.48	85.60	21.40
8	Electricity	9.47	11.97	10.97	12.01	44.42	11.11
9	Rent	85.00	85.00	85.00	85.00	340.00	85.00
10	Petrol	17.27	18.43	21.57	20.87	78.14	19.54
11	Car	19.00	17.00	21.49	26.93	84.42	21.11
12	Total	192.67	191.79	208.86	214.86	808.18	202.05

To select the whole spreadsheet, use the mouse to drag the cursor across the entire sheet or click **Edit** and **Select All** from the menu bar. (Or use the keyboard **Ctrl+A**, i.e. hold down the **Ctrl** key and press **A**.)

Inserting and Deleting Rows and Columns

Often, after keying in the layout of a spreadsheet, an extra row or column is needed. These can be inserted using the drop-down **Insert** menu on the spreadsheet menu bar.

To insert a row, first select the row *below* where the new row is to appear, then click **Insert** and **Insert Row**. To insert a new column, first select the column to the *right* of where the new column is to appear. Then click **Insert** and **Insert Column**.

For example, to add another week's spending figures after **Week 4**, we would place the cursor somewhere in column **F** and then select **Insert** and **Insert Column**. Both the menu and the newly inserted blank column are shown below.

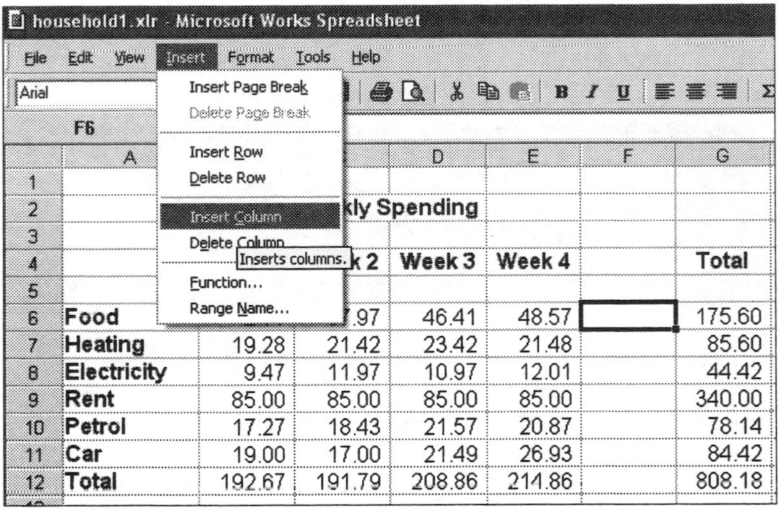

As can be seen from the **Insert** menu above, there are also **Delete Row** and **Delete Column** options.

Entering and Formatting Numbers

You enter the numbers for your spreadsheet by simply typing them in - the program is able to differentiate between numbers and the text or labels already entered. However, spreadsheets allow numbers to be formatted in many different ways. In this example we might want to add a £ sign and use a fixed number of decimal places after the point, as shown below.

When entering numbers representing money into a spreadsheet *do not type a £ sign*, otherwise the program will treat the cell's contents as text and no calculations will be possible. Simply type the raw numbers, without adding any extra 0s or decimal points. Then select or highlight all of the numbers. Now click on the **Currency** icon on the spreadsheet toolbar (shown on the right). This will automatically insert the **£** sign and format the numbers to **2 decimal places** as shown below.

household1.xlr - Microsoft Works Spreadsheet					
File Edit View Insert Format Tools Help					
Arial ▼ 10 ▼ □ ☞ ■ ⏏ ▤ ✂ ▤ ▦ **B** *I* U ▤					
E14					
	A	B	C	D	E	F
1						
2			**Weekly Spending**			
3						
4			**Week 1**	**Week 2**	**Week 3**	**Week 4**
5						
6	**Food**	£42.65	£37.97	£46.41	£48.57	
7	**Heating**	£19.28	£21.42	£23.42	£21.48	
8	**Electricity**	£9.47	£11.97	£10.97	£12.01	
9	**Rent**	£85.00	£85.00	£85.00	£85.00	
10	**Petrol**	£17.27	£18.43	£21.57	£20.87	
11	**Car**	£19.00	£17.00	£21.49	£26.93	
12						

Practice Exercise

Entering Labels and Data and Formatting Cells

You may wish to use the data on page 192 or make up your own data in order to follow this exercise.

1   Start up the spreadsheet program and open a blank spreadsheet.

2   Enter the title of the spreadsheet and the labels **Week 1**, etc. and **Food**, etc. If necessary increase the column width by dragging the dividing line at the top of the appropriate columns as shown on page 188.

3   Centre the labels **Week 1**, etc. by clicking at the beginning of the row then clicking the centre icon on the toolbar. Similarly you could make the labels bold.

4   Now enter the figures without adding a £ sign. You need not add 00's after the decimal point. Format the numbers by selecting all of the number cells and clicking the **Currency** icon on the spreadsheet toolbar. You should see a similar result to the spreadsheet on page 192.

5   Now save the spreadsheet with a suitable name such as **Weekly Spending**. (Then it can be retrieved later for the work on calculations that follows).

6   Make a printout on paper.

If you have time, experiment with the various cell formatting options obtained from the **Format** option on the spreadsheet menu bar. Also make sure you can edit the contents of a cell and insert and delete rows and columns.

Calculated Cells

The general method of performing calculations is:

- Select the cell in which the answer is to appear.

- Select the formula from **Easy Calc** or type it in.

- Ensure that the formula and the range of cells are correct before accepting the calculation.

Although the spreadsheet is capable of complex calculations, this shouldn't deter non-mathematicians. The **Easy Calc** feature in the Works spreadsheet reduces most calculations to a simple task of selecting data and clicking the name of the required calculation.

Column Totals

Returning to the **Weekly Spending** spreadsheet shown on page 192, we can easily calculate the totals for each of the week's spending.

B6:B11	X ✓ ?	=SUM(B6:B11)		
	A	B	C	D	E
1					
2			Weekly Spending		
3					
4			Week 1	Week 2	Week 3	Week 4
5					
6	Food	£42.65	£37.97	£46.41	£48.57
7	Heating	£19.28	£21.42	£23.42	£21.48
8	Electricity	£9.47	£11.97	£10.97	£12.01
9	Rent	£85.00	£85.00	£85.00	£85.00
10	Petrol	£17.27	£18.43	£21.57	£20.87
11	Car	£19.00	£17.00	£21.49	£26.93
12	Total	=SUM(B6:B11)			
13					

First enter the label **Total** in cell **A12**. Next the calculation of the total for **Week 1** has to be entered in cell **B12**. There are various methods, discussed shortly, that free the user from actually typing in formulas. However, you need to check that the *range* of cells, which the program automatically assumes, is correct. The convention for a cell range in spreadsheets is usually **B6:B11**, for example.

Method 1 - Easy Calc

1   Place the cursor in the cell where the answer is to appear.

2   Click the **Easy Calc** icon on the toolbar.

3   Select the **Add** function and then click **Next**.

4   Drag the mouse over the range of cells to be added or enter the **Range:** manually into the range box.

5   Check that the range of cells is correct, in this case **B6:B11**. Edit the **Range:** box if it is incorrect.

6   Click **Next** and you are asked to ensure that the cell in which the answer is to appear is correct - edit the cell reference if necessary.

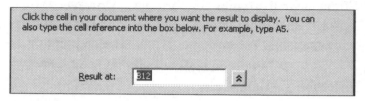

Click the cell in your document where you want the result to display. You can also type the cell reference into the box below. For example, type A5.

Result at: ┌─────────────┐
         │ 312   │ ⌃
         └─────────────┘

7   Click **Finish** to complete the calculation.

Note that the *answer* to a calculation is displayed in a calculated cell, not the formula itself.

Easy Calc provides buttons for the most common tasks such as **Add**, **Subtract**, **Multiply**, **Divide**, **Average** under the heading **Common functions**. There is also a library of additional functions accessed from the **Other** button.

Easy Calc   [?][X]

Click the function you want to use in your formula.

Common functions _____

Add | Adds together two or more numbers
Subtract | using a formula.
Multiply |
Divide |
Average |

Other functions _____

[Other]   Displays a complete list of functions

              [Cancel]   [< Back]   [Next >]

Method 2 - Using the AutoSum Icon

Totalling rows and columns is a frequently needed task, so it has its own icon on the toolbar (called **AutoSum**). Place the cursor in the cell where the first total is to appear (in this case **B12)** then click the **AutoSum** icon. This automatically places the formula **=SUM(B6:B11)** in cell **B12** and in the *entry bar* shown below.

![household2.xlr - Microsoft Works Spreadsheet window showing menu bar File Edit View Insert Format Tools Help, toolbar with Arial 12, entry bar showing B6:B11 X √ ? =SUM(B6:B11), and column headers A B C with row 1]

If the formula and range of cells is correct press the **Enter** key or click the tick next to the spreadsheet entry bar, shown above, to complete the calculation. To cancel a calculation click the **X** shown above.

Any formula such as **=SUM(B6:B11)** can be edited in the entry bar as shown above. First select the cell containing the formula (**B12** in this example) and then click in the entry bar. Click the tick to accept a formula after editing. You can also edit or delete a formula in its cell, after double-clicking the cell.

Method 3 - Typing the Formula into the Cell

This is the traditional method and requires you to know the formula for the operation you wish to perform. (Unless you are doing very specialized work it will be generally be simpler to stick to **Easy Calc**.)

Select the cell in which the answer is to appear. Then type = followed by the formula. (All formulas begin with = to distinguish them from ordinary text or labels.) In this example we type **=SUM(B6:B11)** into the cell then press **Enter** or click the tick on the entry bar. Note that you can construct your own formulas using all of the usual mathematical operators. Please also see page 200. Note that multiply uses * and divide uses /. Care must be taken with the use of brackets to ensure the correct order of calculations.

Replication

We should now have the total of the first column in cell **B12**. This is where the spreadsheet appears to demonstrate "learning". Having already calculated one column total, it can apply the same method to the other three columns with very little further assistance.

Place the cursor in the bottom right-hand corner of cell **B12** until a small cross appears, with the word **FILL** underneath. Now use the mouse to drag this cross across cells **C12**, **D12** and **E12**.

9	Rent	£85.00	£85.00	£85.00	£85.00
10	Petrol	£17.27	£18.43	£21.57	£20.87
11	Car	£19.00	£17.00	£21.49	£26.93
12	Total	£192.67			
13		FILL			
14					

When you release the mouse button the answers should appear in the cells along row **12** as shown below.

	A	B	C	D	E	F
	household2.xlr - Microsoft Works Spreadsheet					
	File Edit View Insert Format Tools Help					
	Arial	10				B I U
	G19					
1						
2			Weekly Spending			
3						
4		Week 1	Week 2	Week 3	Week 4	
5						
6	Food	£42.65	£37.97	£46.41	£48.57	
7	Heating	£19.28	£21.42	£23.42	£21.48	
8	Electricity	£9.47	£11.97	£10.97	£12.01	
9	Rent	£85.00	£85.00	£85.00	£85.00	
10	Petrol	£17.27	£18.43	£21.57	£20.87	
11	Car	£19.00	£17.00	£21.49	£26.93	
12	Total	£192.67	£191.79	£208.86	£214.86	

Row Totals

You can use a similar method to calculate the row totals. Start a new column (**F** in my example) and enter the label **Total** in **F4**. Then use **Easy Calc** or one of the other methods to total the first row and place the answer in **F6**. Then use replication by dragging the cross from **F6** to complete the row totals down column **F**.

Averages

To calculate the average weekly expenditure on **Food**, first enter the label **Average** in cell **G4**. Then place the cursor in cell **G6**. Now select **Easy Calc**, as previously described, and the **Average** function, to place the average in **G6**. Replicate the averages down column **G**.

The completed household spending spreadsheet is shown below.

	A	B	C	D	E	F	G
	household3.xlr - Microsoft Works Spreadsheet						
	File Edit View Insert Format Tools Help						
	Arial ▾ 10 ▾						Σ
	D18						
1							
2			Weekly Spending				
3							
4		Week 1	Week 2	Week 3	Week 4	Total	Average
5							
6	Food	£42.65	£37.97	£46.41	£48.57	£175.60	£43.90
7	Heating	£19.28	£21.42	£23.42	£21.48	£85.60	£21.40
8	Electricity	£9.47	£11.97	£10.97	£12.01	£44.42	£11.11
9	Rent	£85.00	£85.00	£85.00	£85.00	£340.00	£85.00
10	Petrol	£17.27	£18.43	£21.57	£20.87	£78.14	£19.54
11	Car	£19.00	£17.00	£21.49	£26.93	£84.42	£21.11
12	Total	£192.67	£191.79	£208.86	£214.86	£808.18	£202.05
13							

Entering Your Own Formulas

Provided you know the correct method you can do any calculation by entering the formula in the cell where you want the answer to appear. First, you must start the formula with the = sign. Here are a few common examples:

=G5+G8+G9	Add together the contents of these cells.
=F5-F6	Subtract the contents of F6 from F5.
=M5*P8	Multiply the contents of these cells.
=D5/D8	Divide the contents of D5 by D8.
=C9*1.175	Multiply the contents of C9 by 1.175 (as in the case of VAT).
=SUM(C3:C11)	Add together the contents of all cells in the range C3 to C11 inclusive.

Creating Graphs and Charts

The spreadsheet is a very efficient way to store tables of figures and to calculate results. However, it's not easy to look at a row or column of figures and draw any immediate conclusions. Presenting numbers as graphs and charts makes it much easier to interpret the figures and to make comparisons *at a glance*. The spreadsheet in Microsoft Works allows all sorts of charts and graphs to be drawn. These include the *bar chart*, shown on the right, which enables different quantities to be compared side by side.

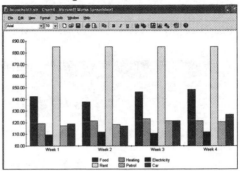

The *pie chart* is used to show how a total quantity is made up of various parts. The relative size of each part is represented by the size of the slice of the pie.

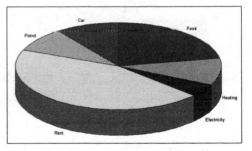

If you've drawn graphs and charts manually you'll know that the hardest part is working out the scales and plotting the points. The charting feature in a spreadsheet program does all of this for you, saving hours of exacting work. You can add titles and labels and apply different colours and shading to the columns or slices. Once complete the chart can be saved on disc, printed on paper or inserted into a page in a word processing document.

Creating a Bar Chart

With the spreadsheet program running and the appropriate spreadsheet table open, highlight the rows or columns of data to be used, including any labels. In the example below I have opened the **Weekly Spending** spreadsheet previously described and selected the four weeks' spending, *including the row and column headings*. (The blank line which was under the row **Week 1**, etc., has been deleted as it causes unnecessary space in the finished graph.)

household3.xlr - Microsoft Works Spreadsheet

File Edit View Insert Format Tools Window Help

Arial   12

A4:E10

	A	B	C	D	E	F	G
1							
2			Weekly Spending				
3							
4		Week 1	Week 2	Week 3	Week 4	Total	Average
5	Food	£42.65	£37.97	£46.41	£48.57	£175.60	£43.90
6	Heating	£19.28	£21.42	£23.42	£21.48	£85.60	£21.40
7	Electricity	£9.47	£11.97	£10.97	£12.01	£44.42	£11.11
8	Rent	£85.00	£85.00	£85.00	£85.00	£340.00	£85.00
9	Petrol	£17.27	£18.43	£21.57	£20.87	£78.14	£19.54
10	Car	£19.00	£17.00	£21.49	£26.93	£84.42	£21.11
11	Total	£192.67	£191.79	£208.86	£214.86	£808.18	£202.05
12							

 Start the charting feature by clicking on the **New Chart** icon on the spreadsheet toolbar. Alternatively select **Tools** and **Create New Chart** from the spreadsheet menu bar. A dialogue box opens, offering a choice from a vast array of different types of chart, as shown on the next page.

After selecting the type of chart you want, you can add a **Chart title:** and switch on effects such as a **Border** and **Gridlines**. The panel on the right of the **New Chart** dialogue box gives you an idea of what your graph will look like. You may find that the small preview graph shown in the panel does not display the data in the way you intend. This can be corrected in the **New Chart** dialogue box after selecting the **Advanced Options** tab. You may need to change the selected radio button as shown below. In the above spreadsheet, the series are **Food, Heating**, etc., and the data goes across in rows.

At this stage it's a good idea to check the organization of the labels and the legend (or key) to each of the columns on the bar chart. However, many of these settings can be altered later after selecting **Edit** or **Format** off the chart menu bar.

When you are happy with the layout of the chart, click **OK**. The sample bar chart based on the **Weekly Spending** spreadsheet is shown below.

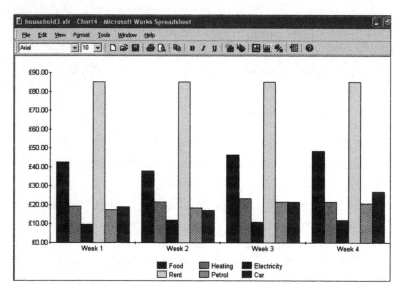

Please note that the bar chart is drawn in its own window with a full menu bar and toolbar across the top. This includes the usual **File** menu with options such as to **Save** and **Print** the chart. You can also change the colours and apply patterns of shading to the columns shown above. With the bar chart displayed, select **Format**, then **Shading** and **Color....** A dialogue box appears allowing you to select patterns and colours for the six series **Food**, **Heating**, **Electricity**, **Rent**, **Petrol** and **Car**.

Creating a Pie Chart

The pie chart is an ideal way to show how various items contribute to a total. The pie chart shown below is based on the spending on **Food, Heating, Electricity**, etc., in **Week 1**.

	A	B	C	D	E	F	G
1							
2			Weekly Spending				
3							
4		Week 1	Week 2	Week 3	Week 4	Total	Average
5	Food	£42.65	£37.97	£46.41	£48.57	£175.60	£43.90
6	Heating	£19.28	£21.42	£23.42	£21.48	£85.60	£21.40
7	Electricity	£9.47	£11.97	£10.97	£12.01	£44.42	£11.11
8	Rent	£85.00	£85.00	£85.00	£85.00	£340.00	£85.00
9	Petrol	£17.27	£18.43	£21.57	£20.87	£78.14	£19.54
10	Car	£19.00	£17.00	£21.49	£26.93	£84.42	£21.11
11	Total	£192.67	£191.79	£208.86	£214.86	£808.18	£202.05

When you have selected the two columns containing the labels and the data, click the chart icon on the spreadsheet toolbar to display the **New Chart** dialogue box shown on page 203. Select the type of pie chart you want. After you click **OK** the pie chart is drawn in its own window with a menu bar and toolbar across the top.

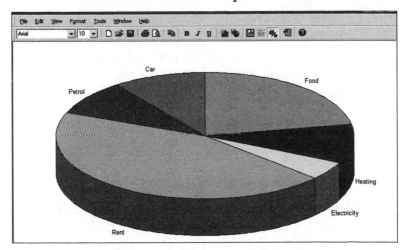

Practice Exercise – Spreadsheets

1   Use **File** and **Open...** to retrieve the spreadsheet which you may have saved previously with a name such as **Weekly Spending**. Alternatively type in the spreadsheet data on page 192.

2   Enter the label **Total** in cell **A12** (or thereabouts).

3   Select the cell where the first column total is to appear, such as **B12**, for example.

4   Use **Easy Calc** or **AutoSum** to calculate the first column total in **B12**.

5   Move the cursor to the bottom right of the calculated cell until the cross appears. Complete all of the column totals by "dragging" the cross along the **Total** row.

6   Now enter a new **Total** label in cell **F4** (or thereabouts) and complete all of the *row totals* in the new column. Use **Easy Calc** or **AutoSum** for the first row total then use dragging to replicate the other row totals down the column.

7   If you have used the spreadsheet data given in this chapter, the row and column totals should be the same as those in the example on page 200. Check the totals and repeat any calculations if necessary.

8   Enter a label for the average column in **G4** (or thereabouts).

9   Select the cell where the first average is to appear, such as **G5**.

10   Click the **Easy Calc** icon and select **Average**.

11   Check the range that **Easy Calc** has suggested.

12 Correct the range, if necessary, in the **Range:** box in **Easy Calc**. (It must not include the **Total** column.)

13 Click **Next** and check that the cell reference given in **Result at:** is correct. Alter the cell reference if necessary.

14 Click **Finish** to complete the first average.

15 Select the cell containing the first calculated average. Move the cursor to the bottom right of the cell until the cross appears. Drag the cross down the column then release to complete the averages column.

16 If you have used the data given in this chapter, the averages should be as shown on page 200.

17 Save the spreadsheet on your hard disc with a name such as **Weekly Spending**.

18 Make a printout on paper.

19 With your spreadsheet open select, i.e. highlight, several columns of data and their labels. Click the chart icon then select a bar chart from the **New Chart** dialogue box. Enter a **Chart title** and look at the small graph to check that the display is correct. Otherwise alter the display after selecting **Advanced**, as discussed on page 203.

20 Click **OK** to display the bar chart.

21 Save the chart and make a printout on paper.

22 Create a pie chart to show a breakdown of the various items of expenditure **Food**, **Heating**, **Electricity**, **Rent**, **Petrol** and **Car.**

23 Save and print the pie chart.

Checklist: Using a Spreadsheet Program

This chapter has covered most of the basic spreadsheet skills. You may wish to use the following tick list to review what you've learned.

Spreadsheet Skills	Achieved
Enter labels and headings and apply text formatting.	
Enter and format numbers including currency format.	
Carry out calculations such as totals and averages.	
Replicate formulas along a row and down a column.	
Edit the contents of a cell.	
Insert and delete rows and columns.	
Save and retrieve a spreadsheet file.	
Print a spreadsheet on paper.	
Create a bar chart.	
Create a pie chart.	
Save and print a chart.	

Creating a Database

Introduction

A database program is used in situations where you might otherwise keep large numbers of records on cards. For example, the patients' records in a medical centre or the customers' records in a business. On a personal level, you could create a database file to keep details of all of your favourite music CDs, cooking recipes, plants or house contents.

The database is far more useful than a stack of cards in a drawer. For example, the database file can be *edited*, i.e. modified, electronically so there are no messy alterations. You can *search* for records fulfilling particular criteria and *sort* into a particular order such as alphabetical or numerical.

A database *file* is a large collection of similar records, saved on a disc. In this chapter, we will look at a file of holiday records. In practice, a database file might extend to hundreds or even thousands of records. The example below shows a small sample of records from a file of holidays.

	Destination	Date	Departs From	Days	Price
1	Canadian Rockies	18/03/2004	Manchester	11	£829
2	Dublin	25/03/2004	East Midlands	3	£145
3	Prague & Vienna	28/03/2004	Birmingham	7	£435

A *record* is one complete row across the list, such as record number **2**, the **Dublin** holiday.

2	Dublin		25/03/2004	East Midlands		3	£145

A *field* is one of the sub-divisions of the record, such as **Destination** and **Date** shown on the previous page. The data in the fields consists of text or numbers or a mixture of both. Databases also allow special field types such as dates and currency, discussed later.

Viewing Records

There are two basic layouts in which database records may be viewed. **List View**, shown below, displays all of the records laid out in a table similar to a spreadsheet, enabling you to scroll down the entire file to browse through the records.

		Destination	Date	Departs From	Days	Price
☐	1	Canadian Rockies	18/03/2004	Manchester	11	£829
☐	2	Dublin	25/03/2004	East Midlands	3	£145
☐	3	Prague & Vienna	28/03/2004	Birmingham	7	£435
☐	4	China	18/03/2004	Heathrow	10	£948
☐	5	Eden Project	19/04/2004	(Local Coach)	4	£185
☐	6	Rome & Venice	29/05/2004	East Midlands	7	£265
☐	7	Monet's Garden	10/06/2004	Luton	4	£159
☐	8	Malta	15/03/2004	Birmingham	12	£259
☐	9	New Zealand	09/04/2004	Stansted	14	£1,549
☐	10	Highland Railways	10/04/2004	N/A	5	£249

Form View enables individual records to be displayed one at a time on the screen, as shown below.

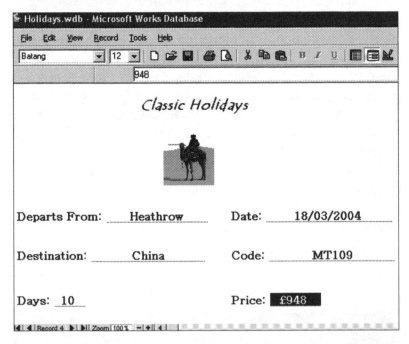

Arrows at the bottom left of the window allow you to scroll forwards and backwards through the records. Alternatively you can use the keys **Ctrl+Page Up** and **Ctrl+Page Down** to move through the records.

The **Form Design** feature (discussed shortly) enables borders and shading to be applied. In **Form Design** mode (accessed by the toolbar icon shown right) the records can be enhanced by inserting objects such as clip art or pictures, as shown in the holiday record above.

Designing a Database File

The database application is one in which careful planning is needed before work even starts on the computer. First you need to decide on the field names, which will be exactly the same for every record. For example, in the holidays file, the field names are **Destination, Date, Departs From, Days** and **Price**. In some files, you might, to save typing time, wish to use codes for data which is often repeated such as **M** for **Male** and **F** for **Female**. Once you have completed the planning of your field names you can start the program and begin setting up the new file.

Database Wizards

In the case of the Microsoft Works database, start the **Task Launcher** by double-clicking the **Microsoft Works** icon (shown left) on the Windows desktop. Then select **Works Database** from the list of programs as shown below.

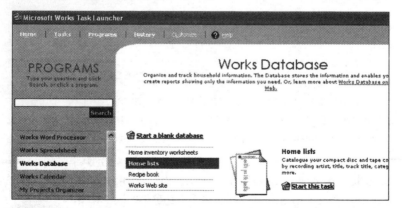

There are some sample database wizards already set up, such as **Home inventory worksheets** and **Recipe book**.

You can look at these by selecting the title, e.g. **Home lists** and then clicking **Start this task**. The database wizard opens, as shown below.

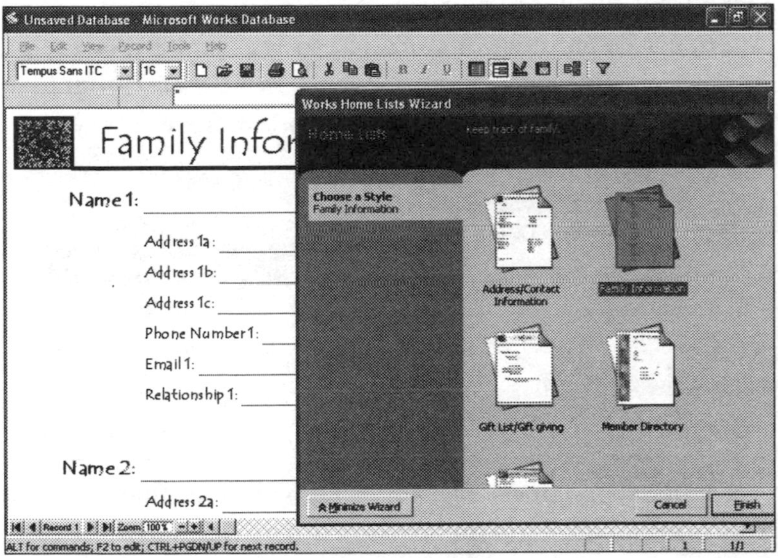

On the right of the wizard above there are several examples of **Home Lists** including **Family Information**. Choose one of these, click **Finish** and a database file opens up as shown on the left above. The field names such as **Name1** above are already in place. All you have to do is to enter the actual data, such as the names and addresses, in this example.

The database wizards in Microsoft Works are worth looking at for ideas about presentation. They are also useful if you need to create a database file on the specific topics covered by the samples. However, the wizards don't enable you to set up your own database applications from scratch, tailor made for a particular subject.

Creating a New Database File

To create a new database of your own in Microsoft Works you need to click **Start a blank database** from the **Task Launcher** shown previously.

Alternatively you can go straight to the database program from the Windows menus using **start**, **All Programs**, **Microsoft Works** and **Microsoft Works Database**.

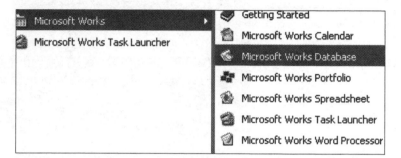

Click **Blank Database** from the dialogue box that appears. This opens the **Create Database** dialogue box shown below.

The **Create Database** dialogue box shown on the previous page is used to enter the field names and also specify the **Format** of the data, such as **General, Number, Date**, etc.

You simply type in your first **Field name:**, such as **Destination**, replacing the name **Field1** in the slot. If later you find a make a mistake or wish to change the field name or format, you can return and make alterations.

Please note that field names (**Destination, Date**, etc.) can be up to 15 characters long. In the **Holidays** file, the first field name, **Destination**, is entered and the radio button next to **General** is left switched on. The **General** format aligns letters on the left and numbers on the right. Then click **Add** and enter the next field name, **Date** and this time select **Date** as the format. Choose from one of the several date formats available, shown on the right below.

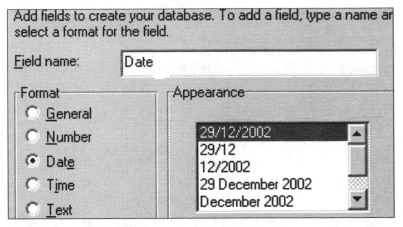

The **Days** field is set to the **Number** format. This will allow the database to be searched for, say, holidays of less than 5 days or more than 10, for example. As holidays are all whole days, in this case the field can be set to no decimal places as shown for the **Price** field on the next page.

The **Price** field must also be in the **Number** format, since you might wish to produce a list of holidays sorted into numerical order of price. Or you might want a printout of all holidays in answer to a query such as "Which holidays are priced at less than £400?" So the **Price** field is set to the **Number** format by switching on the appropriate radio button. This displays a choice of numerical formats and also an opportunity to alter the number of **Decimal places**. In this case the currency format with a **£** sign is chosen, as shown below.

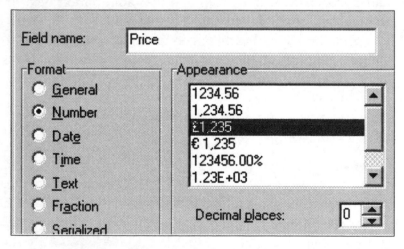

If you want to include pence in the data in the price field, set the **Decimal places:** to **2** by clicking the arrows shown above on the bottom right of the graphic.

This completes the entry of the field names for this simple file of holiday records. Please note that the structure of the records just created is not set in stone. After the initial creation of the file, you can always return and edit the field names and insert or delete fields whenever necessary.

Entering the Data

Having created a database record structure with a number of fields of various formats, click **Done**. This closes the **Create Database** dialogue box and opens up the database in **List View** as shown below. The field names for the new file are displayed across the top with a grid of blank cells underneath, ready for you to start typing in the records.

Entering data into the cells of the database is similar to entering data into the spreadsheet table as discussed in the previous chapter. After typing the data into the first field, pressing **Enter** moves the cursor down the column to the record below. Alternatively move across from left to right using the **Tab** key or move in any direction using the four arrow keys or the mouse.

You can alter the width of the columns for each field by dragging on the vertical line between two adjacent field names such as **Destination** and **Date** (similar to the method for the spreadsheet shown on page 188).

Correcting Mistakes

You can always go back to a cell to edit the data. Double-click the cell or click in the entry bar at the top of the screen.

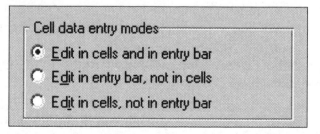

After editing a cell, click the tick on the left of the entry bar shown above or press **Enter**. You can choose where editing may take place by selecting **Tools** and **Options...** and the **Data Entry** tab.

By default the data can be edited in the cells and in the entry bar as shown above.

Alignment of Data

You can alter the alignment of data in a cell. When entering data in the **General** format, letters are aligned on the left and numbers on the right. To alter the alignment of the data in an entire field, such as **Departs From** shown below, first select the appropriate field by clicking in the field name at the top of the column. Now select **Format** and **Alignment...** from the menu bar.

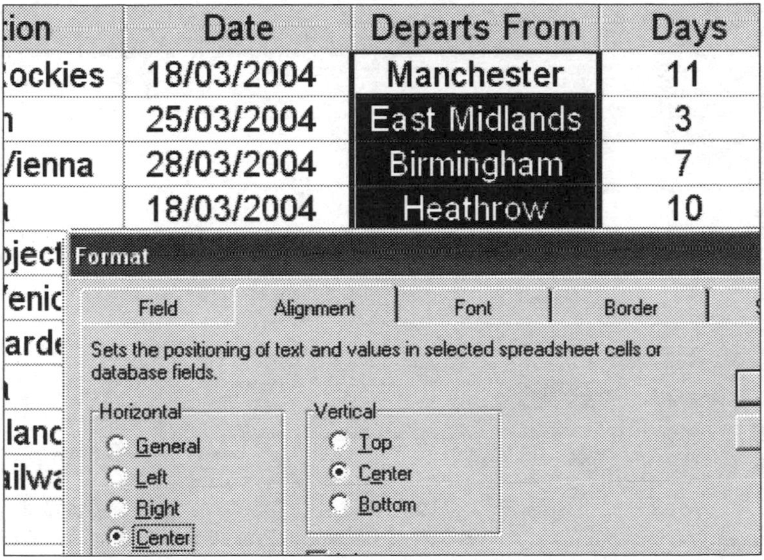

Then choose the alignment you want, **Left**, **Right**, **Center** etc., by switching on the appropriate radio button.

£ Sign

Please note that when entering the data in the **Price** field in the holidays file, having already selected a currency format which includes a £ sign, there is no need to type a £ sign. In this case the £ sign is entered automatically.

Saving a Database File

It's a good idea to save the database as a file on disc at an early stage and subsequently at regular intervals during the entry of data. This doesn't take long and can prevent the loss of hours of work - especially when creating large databases. (The need to create backup or duplicate copies of important files is discussed later in this book).

Select **File** and **Save As...** from the menu bar.

Save As				? X
Save in:	Holidays	▼	← 🗀 ➔ 📷▼	
Holidays.wdb				
File name:	Holidays.wdb			Save
Save as type:	Works DB (*.wdb)	▼		Cancel
	☐ Create Backup Copy			Template...

The first time you save the file you will need to enter a suitable file name, such as **Holidays**. The database extension **.wdb** is supplied automatically.

Further saving of the file can be achieved quickly and easily by simply clicking on the disc icon on the database toolbar, shown left.

Retrieving a Database File

A file can be retrieved using **File** and **Open...** from the menu bar. Highlight the file name and click **Open**, as shown below.

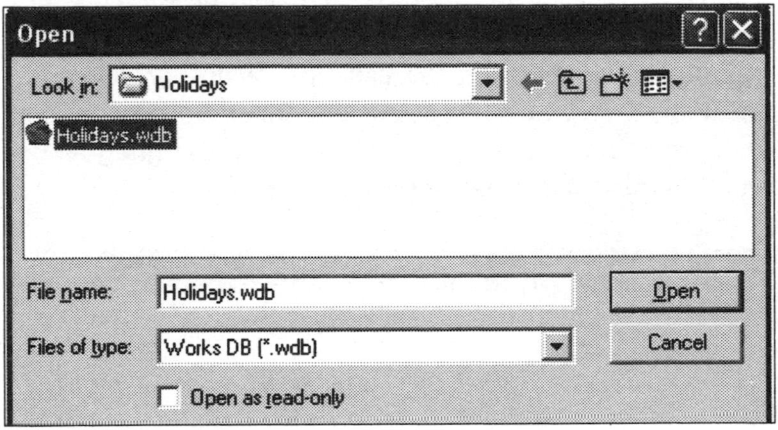

The database file is displayed on the screen as shown below in **List View**. You can scroll up and down the list and check the records.

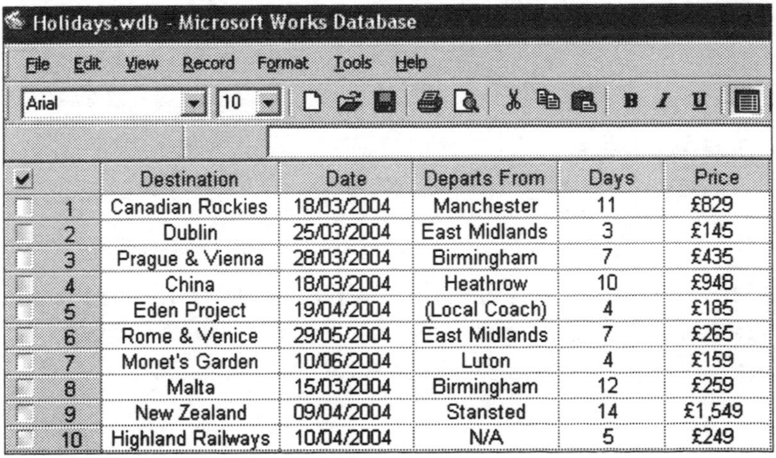

Printing a Database File

You might wish to make a printout using the normal **File** and **Print...** from the menu bar, as in most applications. However, if you print a file on paper with the default settings, you may find there are no field headings or grid lines printed. In Microsoft Works, to switch these on before printing on paper, from the database menu bar select **File** and **Page Setup....** Now select the **Other Options** tab and make sure there are ticks in the boxes next to **Print gridlines** and **Print record and field labels** as shown below.

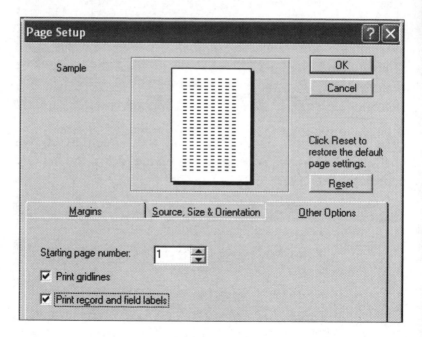

Next time you print the file on paper the field names and gridlines should be printed as well as the actual records.

Editing a Database File

Editing the Data

After reviewing the file you may need to correct data in the cells. As described during the section on entering the records, the data in any field can be edited in the cell after double-clicking the appropriate cell. Or you can select the cell then edit the data in the **Entry bar** near the top of the screen as shown on page 218.

Editing the Field Names

If you want to change a field name or format, click a cell anywhere in the field. Then select **Format, Field...** and change the **Field name:** on the resulting **Format** dialogue box which appears. You can also change the **Format** at this stage i.e. **General, Number,** etc.

When you have finished editing, click **OK** to return to the database which should include the changes you have made.

Inserting Fields and Records

Frequently, after entering all of the data, you may decide one or more extra fields are necessary. Select the field next to where you want to insert a new field. From the menu bar click **Record** and **Insert Field** then either **Before...** or **After...** as shown below.

Record	Format	Tools	Help

Insert Record		🖫 🖨 🗋 ✂ 📋 📋 **B** *I* U 🔳
Delete Record		

Insert Field ►	1 Before...	om	Days	Price
Delete Field	2 After...	ter	11	£829
Sort Records...	04	East Midlands	3	£145

The **Insert Field** dialogue box then appears, allowing you to enter the field name and select the format for the new field. Click **OK** to return to the database file with the new field name inserted and a blank column ready for the new data.

Inserting a new record is done by clicking anywhere in the record *below* the required position for the new record.

 Then select **Record** and **Insert Record** from the menu bar as shown above, or click the icon on the database toolbar.

Deleting Fields and Records

Place the cursor anywhere in the field to be deleted. Select **Record** then **Delete Field** from the menu bar as shown above. Click **OK** in response to **Permanently delete this information?** and the entire field is removed. To delete a record, click anywhere in the record then use the **Delete Record** option in the **Record** menu shown above. All of the above operations can be cancelled using **Edit** and **Undo**.

Form View and Form Design

List View discussed previously allows you to view and print all of the records in horizontal rows in a table format.

Form View presents one record on the screen at a time in a vertical format.

Form Design is a view which allows you to make alterations to the layout of **Form View** and to insert labels and pictures.

Switching between **List View, Form View** and **Form Design** is achieved by clicking on the toolbar icons shown above and on the right of the toolbar below. Alternatively click **View** on the menu bar and then choose the required view.

In **Form Design** (shown below) you can move the fields about by dragging and dropping with the mouse. Any field can be selected then formatted with fonts, borders and shading, using **Format** on the database menu bar.

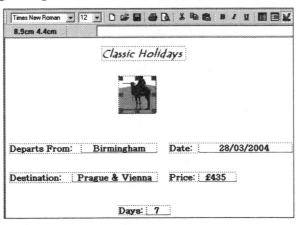

Descriptive headings and labels can be added to the **Form Design** from the **Insert, Label...** option on the menu bar.

After clicking **Insert**, the label is placed on the **Form Design** at the current cursor position. It can be moved to a different position by dragging and dropping, then formatted with a fonts, border and shading.

Various objects can be inserted into the **Form Design** using the **Insert** menu. For example, by selecting **ClipArt...** you can choose a picture from the Works **ClipArt Library**. After inserting the picture into the **Form Design** it can be moved to its final position and resized. When you have finished the **Form Design**, click the icon, shown right, to return to **Form View**. You should see your new design with the data for one of the records inserted as shown on page 211.

Move through the records using the arrows at the bottom. The data for each of the records in turn is infilled into the new form design.

Searching a Database File

One method of searching a large database might be to scroll through the file in **List View**, looking for records which match the required criteria. However, a database program such as the one in Microsoft Works provides fast and sophisticated methods of searching for particular records. In the holiday file, for example, we might wish to find all holidays departing from the East Midlands Airport.

The criteria for the search are set up in a **Filter** and this can be saved with its own name then retrieved and used again. The first part of a search is to set up the filter. With the database open, you can select the **Filter** dialogue box from **Tools** and **Filters...** on the menu bar or from the **Filter** icon on the toolbar, shown right and below.

First you are required to enter a name for the filter. As several other filters may be created for this database, try to use a meaningful **Filter Name**.

After you click **OK** the **Filter** dialogue box opens up as shown on the next page.

The **Filter name:** slot below shows the current filter, **East Midlands**, and also allows previously saved filters to be selected from the drop-down menu.

The **Field name** slot allows you to select the field or fields on which the search is to be based. In a complex search involving more than one field, you would complete 2 or more rows across the **Filter** dialogue box. In the drop-down **Comparison** menu shown in the **Filter** dialogue box above (middle), you select the method by which the records are to be compared with the search criteria. In this example we need to use **is equal to**.

Finally we need to enter our search criteria **East Midlands** in the **Compare To** slot. A second line has been added above to find **East Midlands** holidays where the **Price is less than £200**.

When you have completed setting up all of the criteria, click the **Apply Filter** button. Almost immediately you are presented with the database file showing the reduced set of records produced by the filter.

Sorting Records in a Database File

Sorting involves arranging records in alphabetical or numerical order, based on a particular field or fields. For example, when looking at a list of names or places, it is convenient if they are listed in alphabetical order. The sorting feature in the Works database is invoked from **Record** on the menu bar, then **Sort Records...**. This opens up the **Sort Records** dialogue box shown below,

$\frac{A}{Z}\downarrow$ **Sort Records...**

in which you specify the fields to be sorted and either **Ascending** or **Descending** order.

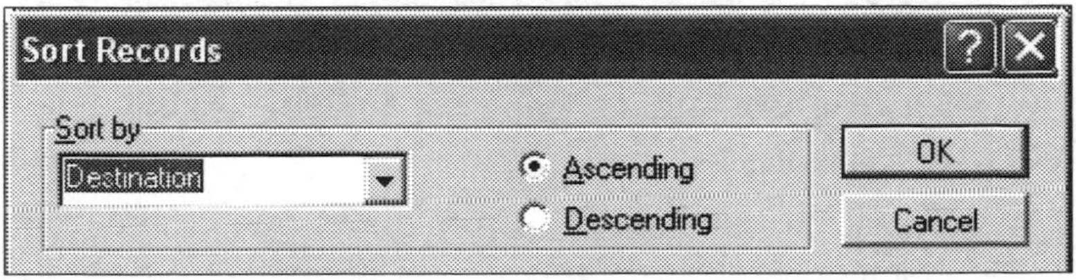

```
Sort Records                                    ? X

Sort by
Destination              ▼      ⦿ Ascending        OK
                                ○ Descending       Cancel
```

In this example, the holidays are sorted into alphabetical order of **Destination**. When you click **OK**, the following sorted list is produced:

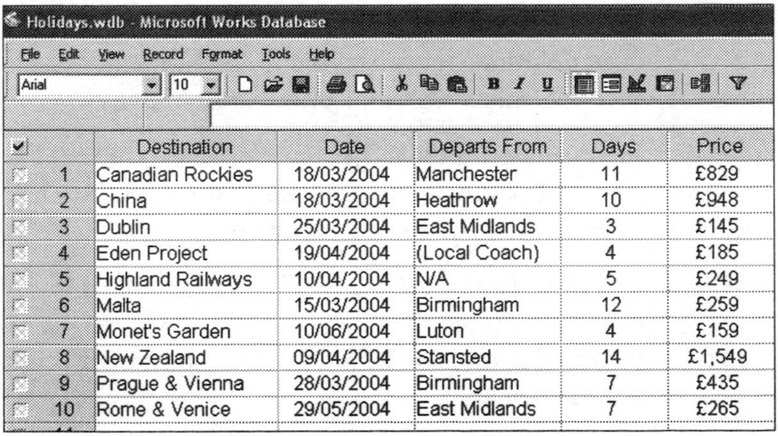

Holidays.wdb - Microsoft Works Database

File Edit View Record Format Tools Help

Arial   ▼ 10 ▼

✓		Destination	Date	Departs From	Days	Price
☒	1	Canadian Rockies	18/03/2004	Manchester	11	£829
☒	2	China	18/03/2004	Heathrow	10	£948
☒	3	Dublin	25/03/2004	East Midlands	3	£145
☒	4	Eden Project	19/04/2004	(Local Coach)	4	£185
☒	5	Highland Railways	10/04/2004	N/A	5	£249
☒	6	Malta	15/03/2004	Birmingham	12	£259
☒	7	Monet's Garden	10/06/2004	Luton	4	£159
☒	8	New Zealand	09/04/2004	Stansted	14	£1,549
☒	9	Prague & Vienna	28/03/2004	Birmingham	7	£435
☒	10	Rome & Venice	29/05/2004	East Midlands	7	£265

229

Practice Exercise: Creating a Database File

1   In this exercise you may wish to use the **Holiday** data given on page 221 or alternatively make up a file of your own.

2   Start up the program ready to create a database file.

3   Enter each **Field name** and **Format**.

4   Click **Done** and start entering the data for the records in the blank database table which appears.

5   As you are entering records, correct any typing errors in the cell or in the **Entry bar**.

6   When you have entered all of the records, save the database with a meaningful file name.

7   Make a printout on paper to include gridlines and field labels.

8   Check the database for errors in the data. Make some changes in the cells, even if there are no actual mistakes. Use both the cell and the **Entry bar** for editing the data.

9   Insert a new *field* and enter a set of data.

10 Insert a new *record*.

11 Practise deleting fields and records. (You can restore them if you select **Edit** and **Undo** straightaway).

12 Save the new version of the file and make a printout.

13 Use **Form Design** to lay out individual records and then check the display in **Form View**.

14 Practise searching for records meeting certain criteria.

15 Sort your file into alphabetical and numerical order on different fields.

Checklist: Database Skills

If you've worked through the last two chapters, you'll have covered most of the basic database skills. You may wish to use the following checklist to tick off those skills you have already acquired and highlight any skills requiring further work.

Database Skills	Achieved
Create a file with numeric and text fields.	
Enter the data and save as a file on disc.	
Retrieve a database file from disc.	
Edit the data, including inserting and deleting records.	
Edit the field names, also inserting and deleting fields.	
Display the file in **List View** and **Form View**.	
Format the file with fonts, borders and shading.	
Use **Form Design** to add labels and pictures.	
Use a filter to find records matching a single criterion.	
Use a filter to find records matching multiple criteria.	
Sort the records on an alphabetical field.	
Sort the records on a numeric field.	
Print records on paper.	

Ideas for Database Files

The following list of possible files may trigger off ideas for your own databases. In each case, the field names are given with a sample record underneath. In practice, you will be able to include many more field names, if you wish.

House Contents File

Description	Date	Manufacturer	Value
Grandfather clock	1847	Henderson	£2500

Trees & Shrubs File

Name	Description	Height	Site
Camellia	Flowering Shrub	8 feet	Light shade

Classic Car File

Make	Model	Year	Value
Jaguar	E Type	1969	£29,500

CD Collection File

Title	Performed by	Genre	Composer
The Four Seasons	The Milton Philharmonic	Classical	Vivaldi

14

Looking After Your Work

The Need for Backups

If you've spent a lot of your valuable time creating any sort of document, whether text, spreadsheet, database, DTP or graphics, the worst thing that can happen is that you "lose" it. Imagine working on a project for several weeks or months then suddenly losing all of the files. The result is exactly the same as someone breaking into a filing cabinet and stealing important documents or a fire which sweeps through a building. The difference is that it's very easy to lose a file or folder saved on a hard disc. As a teacher, I frequently heard remarks like "The stupid computer has wiped my work...". A moment's carelessness when copying or deleting files or a system crash can easily destroy hours of work.

While small files like a letter or simple spreadsheet can be created again very easily, this is not the case with, for example, your autobiography or parish magazine, your family tree or a set of accounts accumulated over a long period. In many cases the value of the data files stored on the hard disc will be far in excess of the value of the computer itself. Imagine working on a book for a year, only to lose the lot - this really has happened.

So it makes sense to devise a strategy for making regular backups, i.e. duplicate copies of your work.

The hard disc inside your computer is the equivalent of the traditional filing cabinet. Apart from data files representing hours of toil, your hard disc also contains all of the systems software such as the Windows XP operating system and applications like Microsoft Office. It's essential that all of your original software packages (including CDs, discs and any documentation) are stored in a safe place, so that the programs can be re-installed later if a disaster occurs.

Ways to Lose Your Data

- The computer or some of its internal components such as the hard disc drive may be stolen.

- You may accidentally delete important files by giving the wrong command.

- Someone may wipe the entire hard disc on purpose.

- The data on the hard disc may be corrupted by a software error or a failure in the power supply.

- The data may be damaged by one of the many computer viruses which can attack your system from various sources, such as a malicious e-mail.

- The hard disc may be damaged by the spilling of drinks or the data corrupted by exposure to a magnetic field after placing it near to another electrical device such as a stereo speaker.

- The computer itself may be totally destroyed by events such as fire, flood, earthquake or explosion.

- After several years' faithful service, the hard disc may reach the end of its useful life.

Although the above list looks pretty daunting, careful use and good backup habits can avoid most of these disasters.

Choosing a Backup Medium

In commercial organizations it's usual to back up an entire hard disc onto special high capacity tapes overnight. This is necessary in business where large numbers of computers are connected on a network. Tape backup was a method I used at one time, using a tape drive unit built into the computer, similar to a disc drive. However, the widespread use of writeable CDs has simplified life considerably and I personally no longer use tape backup systems at all. This is the backup strategy I use and which has served me well in the production of several books - so far avoiding the loss of a single file.

- All CDs (and floppy discs) containing software (Microsoft Windows, Office, etc.,) are stored in a safe place. Should the hard disc need to be re-formatted (thereby wiping it), the programs can be re-installed from the CDs.

- Small backups, such as single files (word processing documents, etc.) are copied onto floppy discs.

- Larger backups are copied onto a CD. For example, one CD can easily accommodate several books, such as this one. Windows XP has the necessary built-in software for copying files onto a CD.

- All backup floppy discs, CDs and original software CDs are kept in a different room (preferably in a different building) from the one in which the computer is based. If there is a fire or someone steals the computer, you will still have copies of your precious work.

Backing Up to a Floppy Disc

The floppy disc is a convenient way to make a backup of a small amount of data such as a single file. It is also a convenient way of exchanging files between friends and colleagues. The disadvantage of the floppy disc is that its capacity is only 1.44MB.

Formatting a Floppy Disc

Before you can use a floppy disc it must be prepared by a process known as *formatting*. This process can also be used to rejuvenate (and sometimes repair) a used floppy disc. To format the floppy disc, place the disc in the floppy disc drive and select **My Computer** from the **start** menu. Right-click over the floppy disc drive icon which appears and select **Format...** from the pop-up menu as shown below.

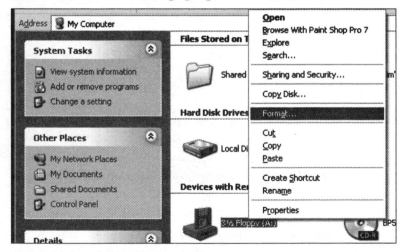

Click **Start** from the next menu and the disc will be formatted ready for use. A **Quick** format is available to remove files from floppy discs which have been formatted before and are known to be undamaged.

Copying a File to a Floppy Disc Using Send To

Open up the **Windows Explorer** or **My Computer**. Now right- click over the file (or folder) you wish to copy. This brings up the menu shown below.

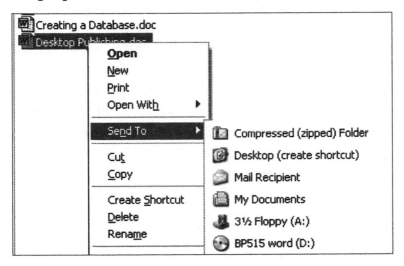

From the **Send To** menu shown above, select **3½ Floppy (A:)**. The file is then copied to the floppy disc, with progress indicated by the window shown below.

Backing Up Your Work to a CD

Many new computers are now equipped with CD drives capable of writing files to a CD. This makes the CD an excellent backup medium. There are two main types of writeable CD, the CD-R and the CD-RW. The CD-R can be written to only once. The CD-RW can be written to many times. I use the CD-R for backup work, for the following reasons:

- The CD-R can cost as little as 50p at the time of writing, especially if you buy a pack of 10 or more.

- The CD has a very useful 700MB storage capacity, compared with the meagre 1.44MB of the floppy disc. You can easily store the equivalent of several books, like this one, for example.

- CDs in my experience are extremely reliable, accurate and virtually indestructible.

A Simple Backup Routine

My own routine is to make a daily backup onto a floppy disc. The next day the latest file can be use to overwrite the previous file on the floppy disc. At the end of each week I copy the whole project from my hard disc onto a CD. You could use a CD-R every day but this creates quite a lot of CDs to handle. Obviously it is important to have an efficient system of *labelling* and storing your backup media in a secure place.

For peace of mind, after backing up important files, it is always a good idea to check that the backup was successful. Try opening the backed up files from the backup media. This can be done using **File** and **Open...** or by double-clicking the file names or icons in the **Windows Explorer** or **My Computer** as discussed on page 242.

CD Writing Software

Earlier versions of Microsoft Windows did not include CD writing or "burning" software, so it was necessary to purchase a third-party product. Two of the most popular packages are Easy CD Creator from Roxio (formerly Adaptec) and Nero from Ahead Software. The CD burning software built into Windows XP is a version of the Roxio software and is an extremely useful backup tool. (Using Windows XP to create *audio* CDs is discussed later in the chapter on Windows Media Player).

Using Windows XP's Own CD Burning Software

Open **My Computer** and double-click the hard disc drive (**C:**) icon to display the folders. Find the files and folders you want to copy to the CD and highlight them. Select **Copy this folder** (or **file**) from the **File and Folder Tasks** menu on the left of the window as shown below.

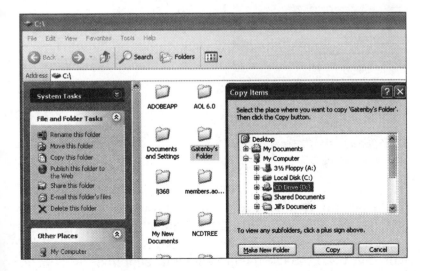

Next select **CD Drive (D:)** from the **Copy Items** window shown on page 239 and then click the **Copy** button.

Alternatively you can use **Send To** as discussed earlier and select the CD drive **(D:)** as the destination.

The files to be copied to the CD are first copied to an image file on your hard disc, prior to copying to the CD. A new window should appear with the files listed under the heading **Files Ready to be Written to the CD** as shown below.

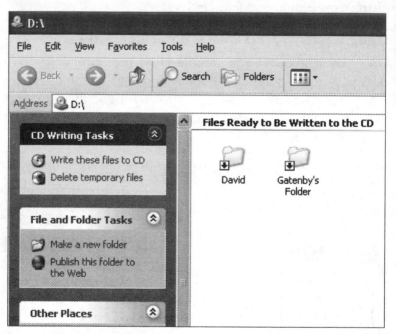

Now highlight the files and select **Write these files to CD** from the **CD Writing Tasks** menu shown on the left-hand side above. This starts the **CD Writing Wizard** shown on the next page, where you are able to give a name to the CD if you don't want to use the default name supplied.

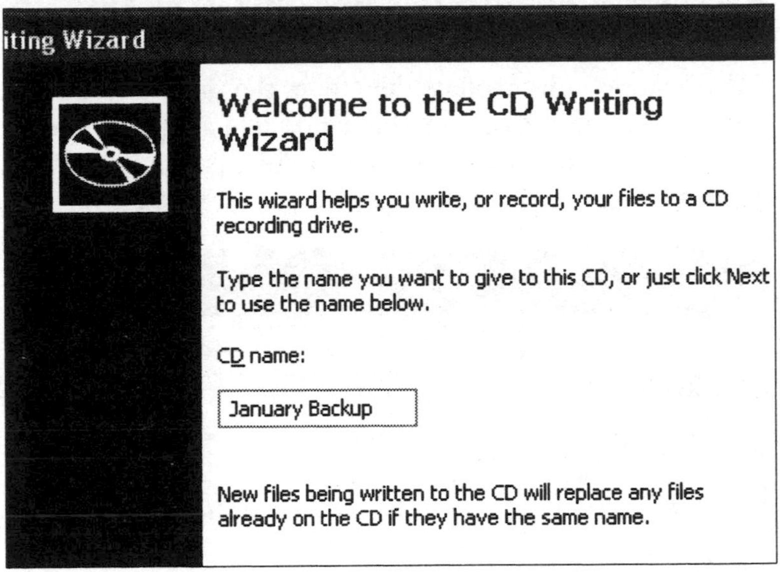

iting Wizard

Welcome to the CD Writing Wizard

This wizard helps you write, or record, your files to a CD recording drive.

Type the name you want to give to this CD, or just click Next to use the name below.

CD name:

| January Backup |

New files being written to the CD will replace any files already on the CD if they have the same name.

After clicking **Next** a window appears showing the progress being made in the copying process.

CD Writing Wizard   [X]

Please wait...

Writing the data files to the CD...

Estimated time left: 15 seconds

After the files have been copied, a window appears telling you that the copying process has been successful. The CD should now be labelled and stored in a safe place.

Recovering Files from a Backup CD or Disc

If you ever need to restore the files you've backed up onto CD (or floppy disc), place the CD in the drive and use the standard **File** and **Open...** commands which appear on the menu bar of most programs. Select the CD drive **(D:)** from the drop-down menu in the **Look in:** bar shown below.

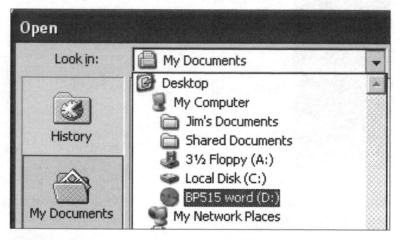

Another way to open a file from a CD (or any other disc) is to display the file name in **My Computer** or the **Windows Explorer,** as shown below.

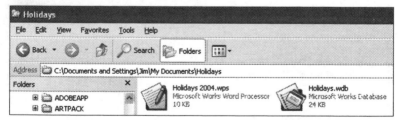

Then if you double-click the file name or icon as shown above, the file will be opened in the program which created it. So, for example, double-clicking a database file will start the database program running and open the database file.

Managing Your Files and Folders

As discussed earlier in this book, you can save your files of work in the default folder **My Documents**, which Windows provides for you. However, when you have created a lot of different files on all sorts of subjects, you may wish to save them in your own system of folders. By placing the files into folders representing different categories this should make your files easier to locate.

As described on page 133, folders can be created after clicking the **Create New Folder** icon in the **Save As** dialogue box. This will place the new folder within the folder currently selected, i.e. the folder named in the **Save As** dialogue box. At the same time you can give the new folder a meaningful name. This will allow you to make up your own system of folders, including *sub-folders* or folders within folders. As described on page 83 and 84, this hierarchical or branching system can be viewed in **My Computer** or the **Windows Explorer**.

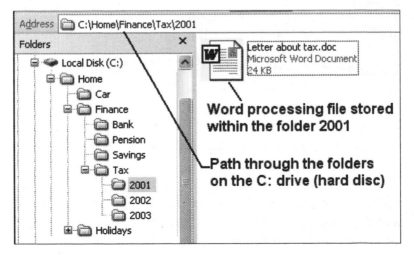

Common File and Folder Tasks

The last screenshot shows the hierarchy of folders and a file displayed in the **Windows Explorer** or **My Computer**. These two Windows features (**Explorer** and **My Computer**) can be used to manage your files and folders. This includes moving files and folders to other folders within the hierarchy and renaming and deleting files and folders. Most of the work in this chapter applies to all recent versions of Windows such as Windows 98, Windows Millenium and Windows XP. Many of these tasks can also be carried out using the new **File and Folder Tasks** pane introduced in Windows XP and this is discussed in detail later in this chapter.

Renaming Files and Folders

A folder or file can be renamed by right-clicking over its name or icon in My Computer or the Windows Explorer, then selecting **Rename** from the menu which appears (shown on the right). Alternatively the folder or file name can be highlighted, followed by selection of **File** and **Rename** from the menu bar across the top of the Explorer or My Computer window. The folder or file name appears in a rectangle with a flashing cursor. Rename the folder or file by deleting the existing name and typing in the new one, then press **Enter**.

Deleting Files and Folders

Highlight the file or folder in the Windows Explorer or My Computer then press the **Delete** key. Or you can select **Delete** from the **File** menu. (The **File** menu can be selected from the menu bar or by right-clicking over the file or folder). When you delete a folder in Windows XP then all of the subfolders and files contained within are also deleted, i.e. moved to the **Recycle Bin**. Some earlier versions of Windows require a folder to be empty before it can be deleted.

To delete files in Windows XP (in the Windows Explorer or My Computer) you can highlight the file or folder and select **Delete this file** from the **File and Folder Tasks** menu on the left of the screen, as shown below. If this menu does not appear, select **View, Explorer Bar** and click the word **Folders** in the drop-down menu, to remove the tick.

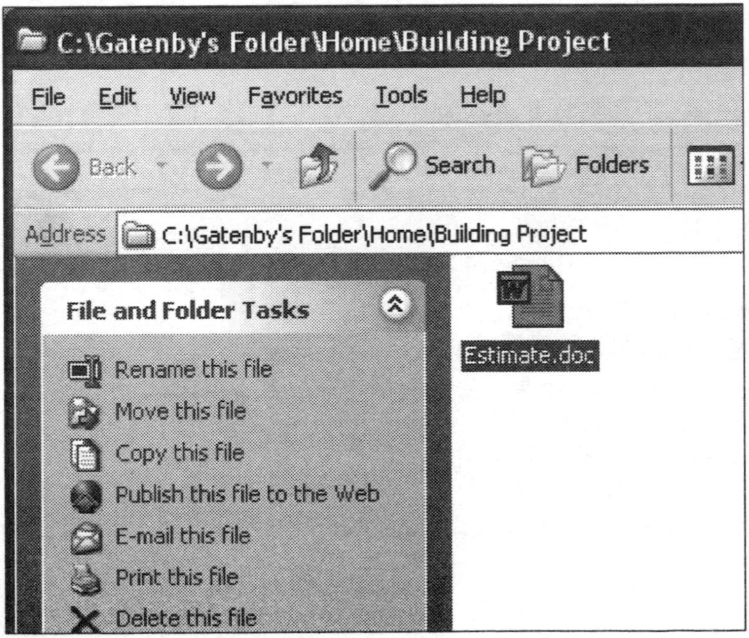

Undoing a Delete Operation

If you make a mistake and delete the wrong folders or files, you can use the **Undo Delete** option in the **Edit** menu (provided you spot the mistake straightaway.) Fortunately files and folders are not lost forever when they are deleted. Windows XP merely transfers them to its **Recycle Bin**. Once in the Recycle Bin files and folders can be left for a time, but as they are still taking up hard disc space they should eventually be permanently deleted. There is also an option to restore files from the Recycle Bin to their original location on the hard disc.

The Recycle Bin

The Recycle Bin is invoked by clicking its icon on the Windows Desktop. It is effectively a folder into which all deleted files are initially sent. As shown below, you can view the contents of the Recycle Bin at any time by clicking its icon on the Windows Desktop.

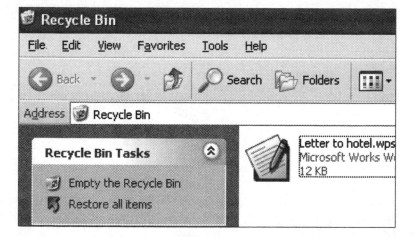

Files which have been "deleted" remain in the Recycle Bin until you decide to empty it. This is done by selecting **Empty the Recycle Bin** from the **Recycle Bin Tasks** shown in the previous screenshot or by selecting **File** then **Empty Recycle Bin** off the menu bar at the top of the Recycle Bin window. The Recycle Bin should be emptied regularly since files in the Recycle Bin are still taking up disc space. Individual files can also be highlighted and deleted.

Should you wish to reinstate files which have been consigned to the bin, open up the Recycle Bin window by clicking its icon on the Windows Desktop. Then highlight the file to be restored and select **Restore this item** from the **Recycle Bin Tasks** menu. Alternatively select **File** and **Restore** from the menu bar for the Recycle Bin. The files will be restored to their original locations on the hard disc.

Moving and Copying Files and Folders

The following tasks are described in the context of files, but the methods apply equally to folders.

Moving a file deletes the file from its original location and places it in a new location.

Copying a file places a replica of the file in a new location and leaves the original edition of the file in the original location.

Files may be copied or moved between different locations on the same hard disc, between two hard discs in the same computer or between different media such as hard and floppy discs.

Dragging and Dropping

A common copying method is to drag the file or folder and drop it over the new location. Different results are obtained depending on whether you are dragging and dropping to the same or a different medium:

- The file is *moved* if it is dragged and dropped into a different location on the *same* hard disc.

- The file is *copied* if it is dragged and dropped onto a different disc drive.

To *copy* files within the same hard disc the **Control** key (marked **Ctrl**) must be held down while dragging with the left-hand mouse button.

Files and folders can be copied in the Windows Explorer or My Computer. You can copy between different locations on the main hard disc drive **C:** or to and from any other drives such as the floppy disc or CD. Open the Windows Explorer and make sure the folders or files you wish to copy or move are visible in the right-hand panel. If you can't see the resources such as the hard disc (**C:**), floppy disc drive (**A:**), etc., in the left-hand panel as shown below, select **View**, **Explorer Bar** and make sure **Folders** is ticked.

Now highlight the file(s) or folder(s) to be copied or moved. (To highlight multiple files and folders, hold down the **Ctrl** key continuously while clicking with the mouse.) Next hold down the left-hand button and drag the highlighted files and/or folders to their destination in the left-hand panel. Release the mouse button to drop the files into the new location.

This method would typically be used to copy some files onto a floppy disc or CD in order to transfer the files to another computer.

Using the Right-hand Mouse Button to Copy or Move Files

Drag the icon for a file or folder using the right-hand button on the mouse, then release the button to drop the file over its new location. The menu shown on the right appears, allowing you to choose whether the file is to be moved or copied.

Copy Here

Move Here

Create Shortcuts Here

Cancel

You can also copy and move files in the Windows Explorer or My Computer by using the **Edit** menus in the respective windows for the source and destination folders. Select the file(s) then use **Edit** and either **Copy** or **Cut** in the first (source) window followed by **Edit** and **Paste** in the destination window.

The File and Folder Tasks Menu

Windows XP has made many file and folder tasks much simpler. This has been done by the addition of the **File and Folder Tasks** pane on the left of the Windows Explorer and My Computer screens. The **File and Folder Tasks** pane, shown below, can be switched on and off in Explorer or My Computer by clicking **View**, **Explorer Bar** and **Folders**.

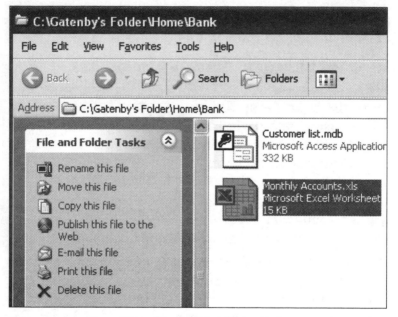

Please note that if a *file* is highlighted in the right-hand pane above, a list of tasks appropriate to *files* appears in the in the **File and Folder Tasks** pane on the left above. If a *folder* is highlighted in the right-hand pane shown above, a list of tasks appropriate to *folders* appears in the **File and Folder Tasks** pane on the left above. This is shown in the two panes on the next page.

Apart from options such as to **Rename** and **Delete**, **E-mail** and **Publish on the Web** as shown on the previous page, files and folders can also be moved or copied very easily using the **File and Folder Tasks** pane.

Moving or copying is made easy with special **Copy Items** and **Move Items** windows appearing when either **Move this file** (or **folder**) or **Copy this file** (or **folder**) are selected. As shown above the same method is used for both *files* and *folders*, depending which has been highlighted in Explorer. The **Copy Items** and **Move Items** windows allow the destination to be selected, as shown below.

For example, the folder called **Tax**, shown highlighted below, is to be moved. **Move this folder** is selected from the **File and Folder Tasks** panel shown on the left below. Then the **Move Items** dialogue box appears enabling you to select the destination for the folder being moved. This could be another folder on the **C:** drive, a floppy disc or writeable CD in drive **D:**. Click the **Move** button to complete the operation. The **Copy** process is carried out in a similar way.

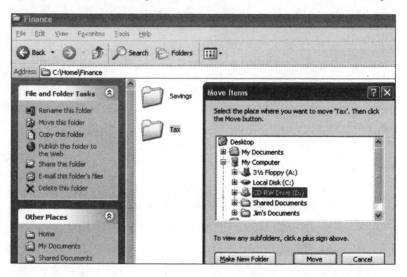

Warning: Don't Re-organize Your Program Files!

Please note that operations to move, delete and rename files and folders should only be used to organize your *data files*, i.e. the work that you have created such as word processing and spreadsheet files and pictures and photographs, etc.

Under no circumstances should you attempt to move, organize or "tidy up" any files or folders which are part of programs such as Microsoft Word or Office, etc. This will stop the programs from working and require the software to be re-installed.

Protection Against Viruses

A virus is a small computer program written maliciously to damage software and data and to cause inconvenience to the user. Unfortunately the files on your hard disc are vulnerable to attack from computer viruses, unless you take precautions to protect them. This means installing some anti-virus software and keeping it up to date so that the program recognizes the latest viruses.

The virus enters a computer system insidiously, often from a rogue floppy disc or an e-mail. If not detected the virus multiplies and spreads throughout a hard disc. Some viruses may only cause trivial damage - such as displaying a so-called 'humorous' message - while others, such as **"Ripper"** or **"Jack the Ripper"**, shown below, can destroy files or wipe an entire hard disc.

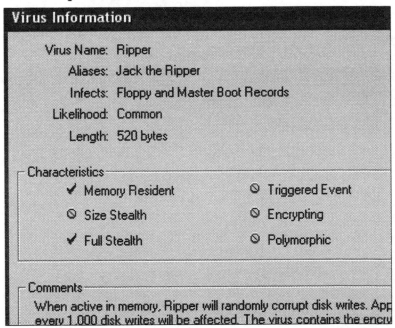

Even when a virus doesn't do any serious damage to files and software, getting rid of it may waste a lot of valuable time - not to mention the anxiety caused if you fear the loss of files which may be very important to you.

Writing viruses is an act of vandalism and can result in a prison sentence. Viruses can exist on floppy and hard discs. They can also reside temporarily in the computer's memory - but they are removed from the memory when the computer is switched off. Viruses do not permanently damage the physical parts of a computer - hardware components such as the memory or the printer.

Viruses can also enter your system from the Internet, perhaps through e-mail *attachments*, the programs or documents "clipped" onto an e-mail (discussed later).

The Norton AntiVirus software package has a scanning program (called Auto-Protect) which constantly monitors e-mail attachments being downloaded to your computer from an Internet mail server.

Great care should be taken when opening e-mails of doubtful origin; if you are suspicious the e-mail should be deleted immediately without opening.

Types of Virus

The File Virus

File viruses attach themselves to *program* or *executable* files. These files (having file name extensions such as **.EXE**, **.COM**, **.SYS**, etc.,) are part of programs like Microsoft Word or Excel. The file virus (also known as the *program* virus) does not infect the *documents* produced using the software, although documents can be infected by the *macro virus* discussed next. (In this context, the term *document* includes not only text produced in a word processor but other types of file saved on disc, such as Excel spreadsheets.)

The Macro Virus

This type of virus has been designed to infect the *documents* produced using programs such as Word and Excel. These programs have their own inbuilt programming language. This allows the advanced user to write small sets of instructions known as *macros*. Unfortunately the virus writers have found ways of writing viruses in the macro language. So, for example, documents produced in programs like Word and Excel can contain viruses.

It's therefore possible for your hard disc to be infected with viruses spread in document files received via the Internet as *attachments* to e-mail (as well as files transferred from another computer via a floppy disc or CD.)

Needless to say, great care must be taken when sending files on a disc or CD to anyone else. If the recipient is a company or organization with a network, there is a danger of a large number of computers being infected. (In theory, any well-run business should have installed its own anti-virus software and systems to stop the import of files from discs and CDs of dubious origin.)

Boot Sector Viruses

The *boot sector* is an area of a floppy or hard disc and contains information needed when the computer is started up or "booted". (The term originates from the expression "pulling yourself up by your own bootstraps.")

Virus Information

Virus Name: Horse Boot

Aliases:

Infects: Floppy and Master Boot Records

Likelihood: Rare

Length: 520 bytes

Characteristics

✔ Memory Resident   ⊘ Triggered Event

⊘ Size Stealth   ⊘ Encrypting

⊘ Full Stealth   ⊘ Polymorphic

Even a floppy disc which contains only *data files* (rather than *program files*) has a boot sector which can be infected by a virus. If an infected floppy disc is inadvertently left in a disc drive when a computer is switched off, next time the machine is "booted up", a virus can spread via the memory and damage the files on the hard disc. (Unless the computer has been set to boot directly from the hard disc).

Stealth Viruses

There are many ways in which the virus writer tries to cause damage whilst avoiding detection. The stealth virus actively tries to conceal itself by making the computer behave normally until it's ready to strike.

Trojans

The Trojan, as its name implies, is a program with an apparently genuine function, but which is really designed to do damage. It is not a virus since it does not replicate itself.

Virus Information

Virus Name: Login Thief Trojan
Aliases:
Infects: N/A
Likelihood: Common
Length: 754 bytes

Characteristics
✔ Memory Resident   ⊘ Triggered Event
⊘ Size Stealth   ⊘ Encrypting
⊘ Full Stealth   ⊘ Polymorphic

One such Trojan takes over a user's e-mail and uses it to send offensive messages - damaging the reputation of the innocent user. Logic Bombs and Time Bombs are types of Trojan which are triggered when a certain event or date occurs, such as Friday 13th. The Michelangelo virus is triggered on the painter's birthday, March 6th. BackDoor is the name of a recent Trojan which enables a hacker to connect to a victim's computer across the Internet. This allows all sorts of malicious damage to be caused such as deleting files and generally wreaking havoc.

At the time of writing there are over 62,000 known viruses, as listed in the Virus List provided with Norton AntiVirus. Hundreds of new viruses are discovered every month.

Anti-Virus Software

The last ten years have seen the evolution of an ever-increasing list of computer viruses. Windows XP does not contain its own anti-virus software. However, several major companies have developed anti-virus software to detect and eradicate virus infection. Three of the leading software packages are Norton AntiVirus, McAfee VirusScan, and Dr. Solomon's Anti-Virus Toolkit. These provide users with regular updates of virus definitions. Then the latest viruses can be detected and dealt with. Methods of dealing with viruses are discussed shortly.

The anti-virus software must find and destroy the existing base of many thousands of known viruses. A small extract from the **Virus List** from Norton AntiVirus is shown below.

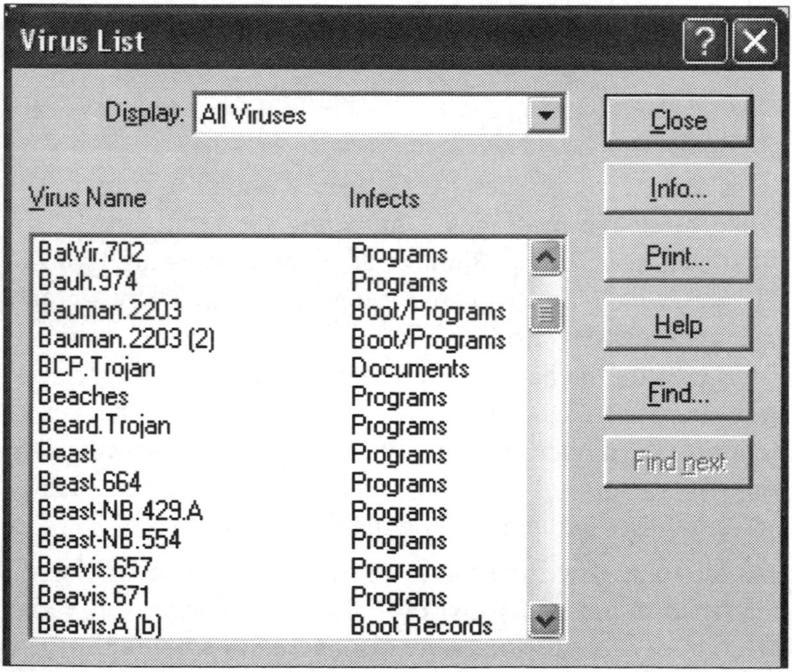

The anti-virus software must also recognize any "virus-like" activity, possibly caused by new and unknown viruses. Virus-like activity would include the computer trying to alter program files - this shouldn't happen during the normal operation of the computer.

Some of the functions of anti-virus software are:

- To continually monitor the memory and vulnerable files, to prevent viruses entering the hard disc and spreading, causing havoc and destruction. The Auto-Protect feature in Norton AntiVirus is a *memory resident* program which is always running in the background.

- To allow the user to carry out *manual scans* to check the memory, floppy and hard discs, whenever it is felt necessary.

- To remove viruses by repairing or deleting files.

- To provide a list of definitions of known viruses, which is regularly updated and distributed to the user, perhaps via the Internet.

It is possible to *schedule* regular scans at certain times:

The Anti-Virus Boot Disc

Should the hard disc become severely infected, a "bootable" floppy disc or CD containing the main virus repair program should be provided in the anti-virus software package. If a virus strikes, the computer should be shut down to stop the virus spreading. Then the computer can be started from the "rescue" or emergency disc and the virus removed from the hard disc.

Features of Anti-Virus Software

When you buy a complete anti-virus package such as Norton AntiVirus, McAfee VirusScan, or Dr. Solomon's Anti-Virus Toolkit, the package will usually comprise a suite of programs providing two different modes of scanning:

First, a scan available "on demand", launched from the Windows menus, like any other piece of software. This is often referred to as a Manual Scan.

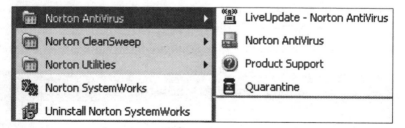

Secondly, a virus scanner which starts up automatically and runs continually in the background, checking files before they are used or as they are received from the e-mail server. Norton AntiVirus runs the Auto-Protect feature from the time Windows starts up.

Norton AntiVirus Help

| Contents | Index | Back | Print | Exit |

Auto-Protect Status

Keep Auto-Protect turned on (enabled) at all times to prevent viruses from infecting your computer. Auto-Protect works in the background, without interrupting your work.

Auto-Protect automatically:

- Detects and protects you against all types of viruses, including macro viruses, boot sector viruses and memory resident viruses and Trojan horses, worms and other malicious code.

- Protects your computer from viruses transmitted through the Internet, checking all files you download from the Internet, including Java Applets and ActiveX controls.

- Checks for viruses every time you use software programs on your computer, insert floppy disks or other removable media, modify or access documents, keeping your system safe at all times.

Disabling an Anti-virus Scanner

Anti-virus scanners which run continually may need to be temporarily *disabled* (but not *uninstalled*) while new software is installed. To temporarily disable the Auto-Protect feature in Norton AntiVirus, you right-click over its icon on the Windows XP taskbar.

When you are ready to switch the auto scanner back on, invoke the above menu again. This will have changed to display the option **Enable Auto-Protect**.

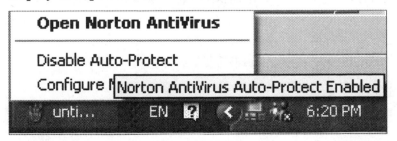

The Manual Scan

This is the main scanning program launched from the Windows XP program menu. The user can select this scan from the menus whenever they wish to check the hard disc or a newly acquired floppy disc. This scanner also carries out the repair of files containing viruses.

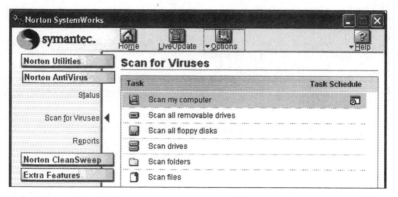

If a Virus Strikes

If you suffer a virus infection, a warning message will appear on the screen, possibly accompanied by an alarm sound. The program can be set up to take a specific action if a virus is found, as shown below.

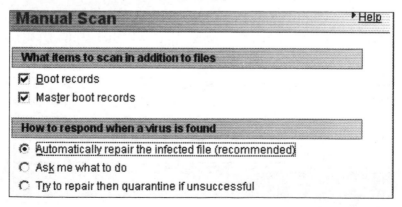

Normally the anti-virus program will try to "clean" the infected file by removing the illicit lines of code which constitute the virus. Otherwise the file must be deleted or excluded.

Quarantine in the previous screenshot refers to a method of isolating unknown viruses, so that they cannot damage files on the hard disc. If Norton AntiVirus is unable to repair or quarantine an infected file, the file is deleted.

The Virus in Memory

This is an extremely dangerous situation, since the virus is ideally placed to damage any files which are run or accessed from hard or floppy disc.

If you suspect there may be a virus in memory:

- Shut down the computer immediately, using the correct procedure.

- Switch off the power to the computer. (This will remove the virus from memory).

- The main anti-virus packages include a disc or CD version of the virus detection/repair program. Use this emergency disc to start the computer and to find and repair any viruses on the hard disc.

In normal use, to prevent a virus spreading on boot-up from an infected floppy disc, the computer should be set to boot directly from the hard disc. If a virus strikes, the computer will need to be re-set to boot from the emergency floppy disc or CD. This involves changing the start-up settings of the computer, which are stored in a special battery-backed memory known as the *CMOS RAM*. A message should appear amongst the text on the screen during startup telling you how to enter the CMOS to change the startup settings.

Updating Your Virus Definitions

Since new viruses are discovered constantly, you are advised to update your virus definition list at regular intervals, weekly say. Norton AntiVirus allows your virus list to be updated automatically when you connect to the Internet or when you select a LiveUpdate from the main window shown below.

Summary: Protection Against Viruses

- Obtain an established anti-virus package such as Norton AntiVirus, McAfee VirusScan, or Dr. Solomon's Anti-Virus Toolkit.

- Obtain and install regular upgrades so that the virus definition list is always up-to-date.

- Always run a virus check on all discs acquired from elsewhere, even brand new packaged software.

- Check any files you distribute on floppy disc, CD or via the Internet, to make sure they are virus free.

- Carry out regular (weekly, say) manual or scheduled checks on all hard and floppy discs.

- Make sure you have a clean, i.e. virus free, write-protected anti-virus boot disc. This will allow you to start the computer after a virus attack.

- Arrange for your computer to boot up from the hard disc, in normal use. (You will need to boot from a floppy disc or CD in the case of a virus attack.)

Using the Internet

Introduction

The scope of the Internet is so large that it's difficult for many of us to envisage exactly what it is. Some people think the Internet is too technical and difficult to use. Undoubtedly many people are put off by all the publicity about the widespread transmission of pornography and child abuse via the Internet. Older people may hear about young "whiz kids" hacking into banks and military establishments and think there is very little in the Internet for them.

Nothing could be further from the truth. The Internet and its billions of "Web" pages can be used for all sorts of everyday, non-technical purposes, which can benefit ordinary people of all ages and backgrounds.

For example, a home computer can be equipped with a cheap "Web" camera which would, for example, allow someone to see their grand children "live" in Australia while talking to them through a simple microphone.

At least one enterprising "retired" couple have set up a thriving business selling porcelain worldwide across the Internet - all from the comfort of their own home.

My own family are certainly not fanatical about the Internet and no-one spends more than an hour or two a week on the Net. However, listed on the next page are some of the things we have used the Internet for in the last year.

One Family's Use of the Internet

- Booked holidays after checking daily vacancies, pictures and descriptions of the accommodation.

- Found up-to-date, high quality information about a serious illness from medical experts.

- Carried out weekly supermarket shopping in 15 minutes, delivered to the door.

- Traced and renewed contact with a cousin in England, not heard of for nearly 40 years.

- Located unheard-of relatives in Canada. Received messages and family photographs by e-mail.

- Printed out a family tree, otherwise unavailable.

- Used the 1901 On-line Census to find details of relatives alive at that time, including addresses, occupations and household members.

- Ordered books and music, delivered the next day.

- Obtained special detailed weather forecasts and flight information for pilots.

- Traced the source of the River Dove in the Staffordshire Moorlands.

- Received accountancy examination results at midnight, almost 36 hours before the paper copy arrived in the letter post.

- "Downloaded" software and music from the Internet straight to our computer.

- Found information about garden plants, shrubs and gardening equipment.

- Opened an Internet bank account offering an above-average interest rate. Transferred funds on-line.

What is the Internet?

The Internet is a network of millions of computers around the world, connected by cables and satellites. The World Wide Web is a collection of billions of pages of information covering every conceivable subject. A *Web site* is a collection of related pages, belonging to an individual person or an organization. The Web pages are stored on many thousands of computers, known as Web *servers*, scattered all round the world. In order to retrieve information from the Web, we must first log on to the Internet and then connect to the Web server containing the relevant pages. A program called a *Web browser* is used to move about the Internet and to view and retrieve information. The most commonly used browsers are Microsoft Internet Explorer (part of Microsoft Windows) and Netscape Navigator, part of the Netscape Communicator suite of programs.

Internet Explorer is shown below displaying a page from a family Web site, accesssed by relatives all over the world.

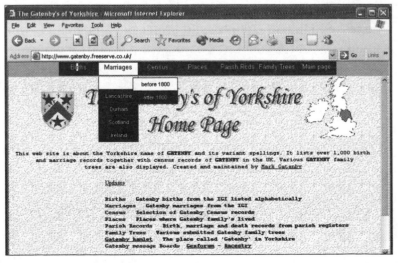

Connecting to the Internet

Most home users connect to the Internet via a device called a *modem* as discussed on page 29 of this book. The modem plugs into your computer either internally or externally. Many new computers are supplied with a modem already fitted. If you don't want to get involved with hardware, any computer shop should be able to install and test a modem in less than an hour. If you are happy to use a screwdriver and connect a few cables, it's a fairly simple task to buy a modem and fit it to your machine.

When you start the computer after fitting a modem, the Windows operating system will detect the presence of the new hardware. Windows may contain the necessary "driver" software to enable the new modem to work with your particular computer. Otherwise you will be asked to insert the CD or discs from your modem manufacturer.

When a modem has been installed correctly you can check for its presence by selecting **start**, **Control Panel** and **Phone and Modem Options**. (You may need to select **Switch to Classic View** in the **Control Panel**). If you double-click **Phone and Modem Options** and select the **Modems** tab you should see your modem listed, like the one shown below.

The purpose of a modem is to convert the information coming out of a computer into a form suitable for transmission across the telephone lines. To connect to the telephone lines you need a spare telephone socket in your home. This can be provided by a cheap plastic dual adapter obtainable from any hardware store.

The disadvantage with the modem connected into your only telephone line is that you cannot use the telephone while connected to the Internet. The BT 1571 service provides a way round this by enabling telephone messages to be recorded while you are using the Internet. Another way round this is to install a separate telephone line dedicated to the computer. This is rather expensive, but may be justified if you are using the computer for business or wish to receive a separate bill for the modem line.

Broadband Connections

Some people find the traditional modem too slow for their use of the Internet. This applies if you wish to download very large files from the Internet to your computer. These files might include software, music, videos or photographs. The answer to the need for more speed is the new Broadband system, introduced by BT and others. Home users of Broadband have a service known as ADSL (Asymmetric Digital Subscriber Line). This converts a standard telephone line into a very fast Internet line. Comparing Broadband to a normal modem line is like comparing a 6-lane motorway to a narrow country lane.

At the time of writing Broadband is starting to take off, after a slow start in Britain. Some rural areas of Britain still can't access Broadband because their telephone exchanges need modification.

To obtain a Broadband connection, you will need to subscribe to a Broadband Internet Service Provider such as BT Broadband or AOL. You will also need to obtain a special *ADSL modem*. Alternatively, if your road has been dug up to install the cables for cable television, there is a Cable Broadband service available from companies such as NTL. This requires a special *cable modem*.

If you are already connected to the Internet with an ordinary modem and want to know more about Broadband, the BT Web site (**http://www.bt.com/**) has details of prices and equipment needed, as shown below.

BT Broadband service
Charged to your BT phone bill[1]:

One-off activation charge £30.00
Monthly rental charge £27.00

BT Broadband equipment
It's easy to purchase equipment from BT when you order BT Broadband. Choose whether you'd prefer to put it on your BT phone bill or pay by credit/debit card. You can also purchase this equipment from other suppliers.

Broadband modem pack £80.00 per pack

Includes 1 broadband modem + 2 microfilters (phone adapters)

You can also enter your telephone number and find out if your local telephone exchange can deliver Broadband.

Here are some of the main features of a Broadband Internet connection:

- Broadband is up to 10 times faster than an ordinary modem, making it possible to view films and music videos "live" from the Internet, a process known as *streaming*.

- Download large files such as software, pictures and graphics from the Internet. These are then saved on the hard disc of your computer.

- Once up and running, the computer is *always connected to the Internet*.

- A monthly fee of about £30 usually includes unlimited access to the Internet.

- You can use the telephone at the same time as the Internet - there's no need for a dedicated line.

Businesses handling large volumes of Internet data and anyone needing to keep up with the latest technology will obviously choose a Broadband connection.

Of course, if you don't need to work with large files, music and videos, or you don't want or can't afford to spend about £30 a month on your Internet connection, you may well settle for a conventional modem. This will be very much cheaper and should be quite adequate for occasional searching of the Internet for information and sending and receiving e-mails.

Although the rest of this chapter was written with the conventional modem user in mind, most of the material is also relevant to users of Broadband systems.

Choosing an Internet Service Provider

Typically you pay the Internet Service Providers for their services by a monthly subscription, although in the last few years there has been a spate of "free" connection services. To avoid receiving enormous telephone bills, connection to the Internet must be available at the *local* telephone rate.

When you start to set up a connection to the Internet using Microsoft's New Connection Wizard, you are presented with a choice of companies known as *Internet Service Providers (ISPs)* such as America Online (AOL) and The Microsoft Network (MSN). Apart from enabling you to browse the World Wide Web and send e-mails, some of these services contain their own news, entertainment and information pages which are only accessible to subscribing members.

Many of the Internet Service Providers offer a free evaluation period (120 hours, say) and you will need to give your credit card details at the outset. If you don't wish to continue at the end of the evaluation period you need to cancel your membership to avoid charges.

CDs containing Internet connection software are often provided free on the front of magazines and in shops and supermarkets. Or you may receive Internet free trial CDs in the post, if your name and address have found their way onto the Internet Service Provider's mailing list.

Some criteria for choosing an Internet Service Provider might include:

- Speed and reliability when connecting to the Internet.
- Telephone access numbers available at *local* telephone rates.
- The monthly or yearly subscription charges.
- The number of e-mail addresses per account.
- The quality and cost of the telephone support service.
- Support for the latest technology, including Broadband.
- In the case of services providing content, the quality and quantity of the pages of information - news, sport, travel, weather, etc., and their value for research and learning.
- The amount of Web space available for subscribers to create their own Web sites and any charges for this facility.
- Parental controls over children's access to inappropriate Web sites.

It's very easy to be confused by the large number of competing deals offered by the Internet Service Providers. A good source of help is the computing press, which regularly publishes helpful comparisons of the various ISPs and their charges. If possible talk to people who have experience of using various Internet Service Providers.

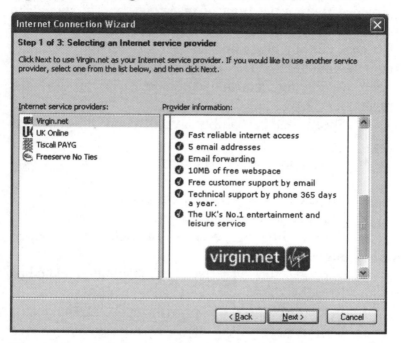

The amount of *free webspace* mentioned above may be important if you want to set up your own family Web site, for example. This might be used to store photographs, viewable by family members around the world. Creating a Web site is not as difficult as it may seem and the subject is covered in the companion volume to this book, entitled "The Internet for the Older Generation" from Bernard Babani (publishing) Ltd, reference BP600.

Making the Connection - An Overview

This section assumes your computer is fitted with a functional modem and is running Microsoft Windows with a Web browser such as Microsoft Internet Explorer or Netscape Navigator. There are several ways to make a new connection with an Internet Service Provider. All of them require you to provide the same information, i.e. your name and address, telephone number and credit card details.

During the creation of the new connection you will set up a *User Name*, i.e. the name you use to log on to the Internet. You will also create or be assigned a unique *Password* and one or more *E-mail Addresses*.

There are several ways to launch the process of connecting to an Internet Service Provider. You can use a free CD from the Internet Service Provider or you can use the **New Connection Wizard** in Windows XP. Additionally, if you know the telephone number of your chosen ISP and have obtained a User Name and Password the connection can be set up manually.

Creating an Internet Connection Using a Free CD

Place the CD in the drive and wait for it to start up automatically (a process known as "autobooting").

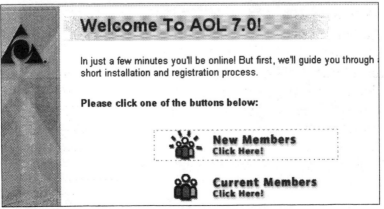

You will be asked to enter a temporary User Name (sometimes also called a *User ID* or a *Reg Number*). You may also be asked to enter a temporary password. This temporary information is normally printed on the cardboard case of the free CD. With this information you will be able to connect to the ISP and enter all of your personal information and credit card details. You should also be able to set up your own personal User Name and Password and also your e-mail address. At the same time make a note of the telephone number for cancelling this Internet account, if it is a time-limited free trial which you may not wish to continue at the end of the trial period.

Using the Windows New Connection Wizard

If you haven't obtained a free CD you can use the **New Connection Wizard** in Windows XP to obtain a list of ISPs in your area. Then choose an ISP and complete the new connection by entering all of your details on-line. The process can be started by launching the **New Connection Wizard** from **start, Connect To, Show all connections** and **Create a new connection,** as shown below.

Choose **Connect to the Internet** from the **New Connection Wizard** shown above.

On clicking **Next**, the wizard presents a choice of the types of connection shown below.

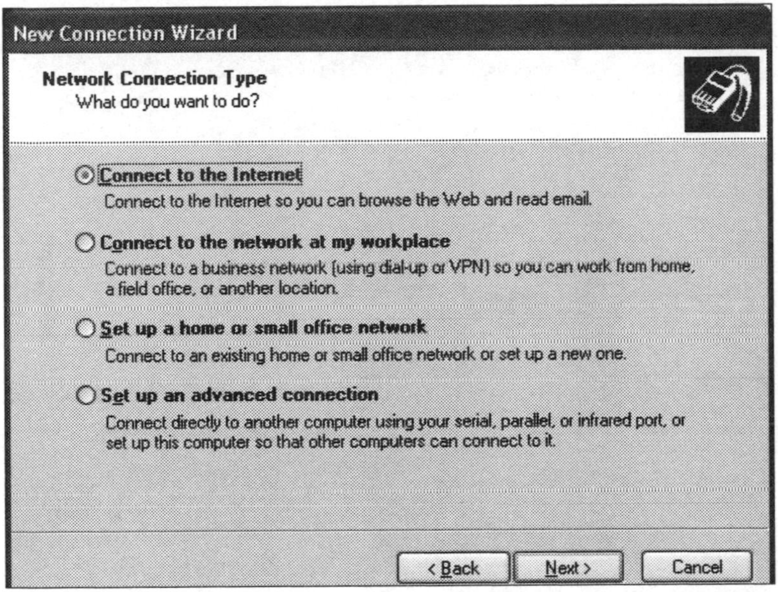

After selecting **Connect to the Internet** and clicking **Next** you are asked to choose a method by which to set up your Internet account.

Select the first option, **Choose from a list of Internet service providers (ISPs)**. This involves connecting to the Microsoft Internet Referral Service for a choice of available Internet Service Providers. Then you must select between:

- **Get online with MSN.**
- **Select from a list of other ISPs.**

Choosing the first option above will enable you to sign-up for the Microsoft Network. Taking the second option above will create a temporary dial-up connection to the Microsoft Internet Referral Service, shown on the next page.

Setting Up an Internet Connection from a List of ISPs

A list of Internet Service Providers available in your area is given, with details of their services.

The left-hand panel above shows a list of Internet Service Providers. The right panel presents the packages on offer by the ISP currently highlighted in the left-hand panel. The support telephone number of your chosen ISP is worth making a note of in case you have any trouble with passwords, etc.

If you select one of the ISPs in the left-hand panel above, then click **Next**, you are presented with a form requesting your name and address, etc., as shown on the next page.

Internet Connection Wizard

Step 2 of 3: Signing up with an Internet Service Provider

To establish an account with an ISP, type the following information. This information is sent only to the ISP selected.

First name:

| |

Last or surname:

Address:

Additional address information:

City:

State or province:

ZIP or postal code:

Phone number:

< Back   Next >   Cancel

After completing the form you will be connected to the ISP server computer where your personal User Name, Password and E-mail are set up and you will be required to give details of your credit card. You may also be able to choose, from a list, the phone number which your computer will use to connect to the Internet Service Provider.

You are advised to check with your telephone company that all Internet connections will be charged at the *local rate*. If you're a BT subscriber, you might wish to add your ISP's phone number to your list of BT Friends and Family frequently-used numbers attracting discounts. At the end of the process you should be able to connect to your chosen Internet Service Provider in order to "surf" the Internet and send and receive e-mails, as discussed in the next section.

Finding Information

Searching for information is carried out using a Web browser such as Internet Explorer, part of the Windows operating system. First you need to launch the browser from the **start** menu or perhaps an icon on the Windows Desktop. Then you will need to enter your user name and password and connect to the Internet. You may also need to click a **Connect** or **Dial** button at some stage.

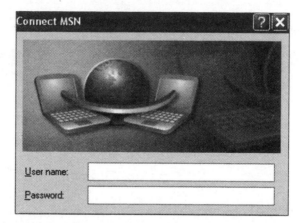

Once you are connected to the Internet, you will see the Home Page of your ISP, such as MSN, shown below.

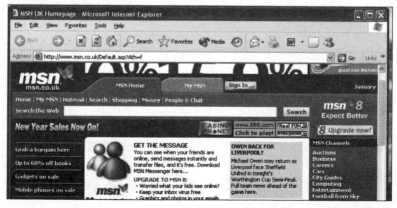

Apart from a large number of advertisements, you can read the latest news items and select pages on topics as diverse as business, health and beauty and travel.

Using a Web Address to Connect to a Web Site

Every Web site has a unique address such as:

http://www.mywebsite.com

If you know the address of the required site, enter this into the address bar at the top of the Web browser as shown below.

When you press **Enter** your Web browser should find the Web site and display its Home Page on the screen. You can then move about the Web site by clicking on various *links*

to other pages. Links are usually words which are underlined and change colour when the cursor is passed over them. Also, when you pass the cursor over a link, the cursor changes to a hand. Pictures are also used as links.

If you find a Web site which you think may be useful in future, a link to the site can be saved using the **Favorites** menu on the menu bar in Internet Explorer as shown above.

To return to the Web site at a later date, log on to the Internet, click **Favorites** on the menu bar and then select the required site in the drop down list of **Favorites**. This should connect your computer to the required Web site.

Key Word Searching

You can find information about virtually every subject under the sun by entering key words into the search slot in your Web Browser shown below.

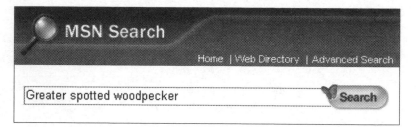

After clicking the **Search** button shown above, the Internet is searched and a list of results is presented as shown below. Each item in the list is an extract from a Web site containing references to the key word or words.

MSN Search

Home | Web Directory | Advanced Search | Submit a Site | My Preferences | Help

Greater spotted woodpecker   Search

Results 1-15 of about 13648 containing '**Greater spotted woodpecker**'   NEXT

WEB PAGES (i)ABOUT

1. Greater Spotted Woodpecker
   Tuesday, 23rd October 2001, West Yorkshire A GREATER SPOTTED WOODPECKER perches for a
   few moments on the post below the bird table.
   www.wildyorkshire.co.uk/naturediary/docs/2001/10/23.html

2. Greater Spotted Woodpecker
   Birds - General Greater Spotted Woodpecker Price £59.95 inc.p&p Please use the back button on your
   browser to return to the shop
   www.ritchies.co.uk/acatalog/wild_grtpecker.htm

3. LVNP Online - Greater Spotted Woodpecker - © Mick Ladner
   Greater Spotted Woodpecker - © Mick Ladner Taken at the Lee Valley with Canon EOS equipment Back
   to gallery index
   www.benszone.co.uk/lvnp/gallery/generated/gswoodpecker.jpg.html

You can see from the previous list of search results that the search found 13648 Web sites all containing references to the words **Greater spotted woodpecker**. One such search result is shown below.

Greater Spotted Woodpecker
Tuesday, 23rd October 2001, West Yorkshire A GREATER S
few moments on the post below the bird table.
www.wildyorkshire.co.uk/naturediary/docs/2001/10/23.html

Clicking on any of the links in the search results (shown underlined above) takes you to a Web site, e.g. **www.wildyorkshire.co.uk/**, etc., shown above.

You may well wonder how anyone can make any sense of 13648 search results. In fact, a search can be narrowed down to eliminate the least relevant results. When we searched for **Greater spotted woodpecker**, the search would find all those Web sites which contained the words **Greater**, **spotted** and **woodpecker** *anywhere* within them. For example, a Web site containing the sentence "I **spotted** a **woodpecker** in **Greater** Manchester" would also match the key words as entered, but would probably not be very relevant. We can avoid this and narrow down the search by enclosing the key words in inverted commas:

MSN Search

Home | Web Directory | Advanced Search |

"Greater spotted woodpecker"   Search

Results 1-15 of about 347 containing '**"Greater spotted woodpecker"**

The inverted commas mean the results will include only those Web sites where the words **Greater spotted woodpecker** appear next to each other and in that order. After carrying out this modified search only 347 Web sites were found. By careful choice of key words for your searches you can eliminate many irrelevant entries in the search results.

Using the Google Search Engine

Apart from the search facilities built into Web browsers like Internet Explorer, there are a number of independent programs which can be used separately. Google is a very powerful, easy to use and popular "search engine" and can be accessed from **http://www.google.co.uk**.

Searching is covered in more detail in the companion volume to this book, entitled "The Internet for the Older Generation" from Bernard Babani (publishing) Ltd, reference BP600.

Tracing Your Family History

The Internet has made tracing your ancestors much easier. For example, typing a relative's name into a key word search (as discussed previously) is quite likely to yield some relevant information. You will probably need to narrow it down with additional key words such as place names. If the person has been involved in sport, clubs, academic research, business or great disasters, for example, you are likely to find plenty of references.

The 1901 Census Online allows you to find family groups living at particular addresses. For each family member you can find their name, place of birth, occupation, age and marital status, etc. You can view copies of the handwritten forms completed by the census enumerators in 1901.

Some useful Web sites including hints and tips about researching family history are:

www.census.pro.gov.uk   **www.ancestry.com**

www.genuki.org.uk   **www.familyrecords.gov.uk**

www.lookupuk.com   **www.rootsweb.com**

You may find that someone has already started a Web site for your family and saved you a lot of hard work. This was the case in my own family, where a very comprehensive site has been created by Mark Gatenby. The site includes a *forum* (shown on the next page) where notices can be posted asking for information about relatives. Through the forum I was able to re-establish contact with a cousin not seen for nearly 40 years and also exchange e-mails with previously unknown relatives in Canada. Mark's site can be found at:

www.gatenby.freeserve.co.uk.

This Web site has numerous pages of family records accessed via menus such as Births, Marriages, Census, Places, Parish Records and Family Trees, as shown below.

From this I was able to view (and print out) my own family tree, "Gatenbys from Guisborough and to Canada".

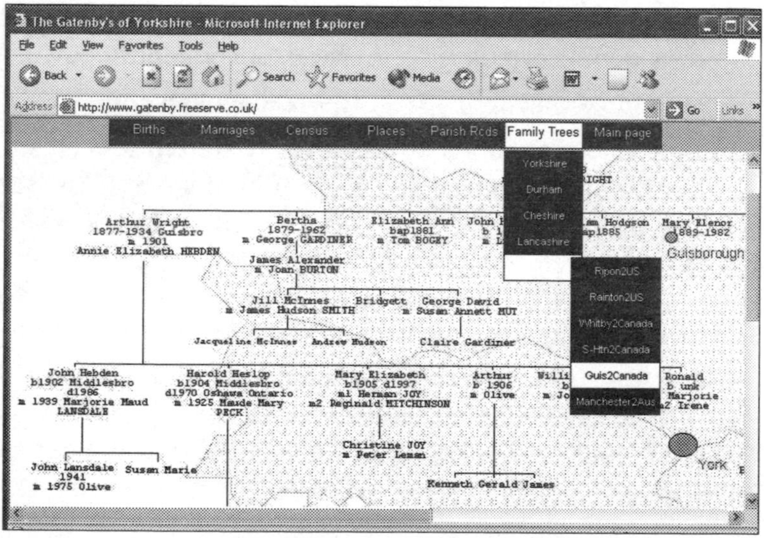

Using E-mail

E-mail is a method of communicating between people around the world. Most e-mails consist of a text message, typically a paragraph or two long. Longer documents can be sent as e-mail *attachments*, as discussed shortly.

Simply type in your message as shown above. You must enter the e-mail address of your intended recipient(s) in the **To:** slot and make an entry next to **Subject:**. **Cc:** and **Bcc:** allow you to send "carbon copies" to other people. After you have typed in your message click the **Send** button and the message will travel *almost instantly* to the Internet Service Provider used by the person receiving your e-mail.

- If your e-mail contact as not currently logged on they will receive your message next time they connect to the Internet and read their e-mail.

- If your contact is logged onto the Internet they should be able to read the message almost immediately.

The new mail will be saved in the **Inbox** of the recipient. From here they can read the message, delete it, print it on paper or save it in a folder.

Windows comes with the e-mail program, Outlook Express. If you subscribe to an Internet Service like AOL, this has its own e-mail program, often called an e-mail *client*.

To start sending and receiving e-mails you will need:

- A computer with a connection to the Internet via a modem.

- An e-mail program such as Outlook Express included as part of Microsoft Windows.

- An e-mail account set up with an Internet Service Provider, including a *user name* and *password*.

- You own unique e-mail address such as **johnsmith@hotmail.com**.

- The e-mail addresses of people you wish to correspond with.

E-mail Addresses

When you sign up for an Internet account you will be able to choose, or be given, your own e-mail address. This is a unique location enabling your mail to reach you from anywhere in the world.

Common types of e-mail address are as follows:

stella@aol.com

james@msn.com

enquiries@wildlife.org.uk

The part of the e-mail address in front of the @ sign is normally your Internet *user* name or *login* name. The second part of the address identifies the mail server computer at your company, organization or Internet Service Provider. The last part of the address is the type of organisation providing the service. In the previous addresses **.com** refers to a commercial company. Other organisation types include:

.edu   education

.gov   U.S. government

.org   non-profit making organisations

.co   UK commercial company

A two-digit country code such as **uk** or **fr** may be added to the end of the e-mail address.

Some of the main features of e-mail programs are:

- Copies of incoming and outgoing messages are saved in special folders such as the **Inbox** and **Outbox** or **Sent Messages** folder. You can also create and manage your own folders for organising your e-mail, as shown below.

<< Hide Folders	Delete	Block	Mark As Unread	Put in Folder... ∨
📁 **Inbox**	■ From		Subject	
📁 Junk Mail	☐ Hotmail Member Servi...		A new year - a new Interne	
📁 Sent Messages	☐ Mark Gatenby		Re: 1901 census Gatenby	
📁 Drafts				
📁 Trash Can				
Create Folder				
Manage Folders				

- An *address book* can be created listing all of your contacts. This saves typing their address every time you send them a message - you simply select it from the address book and click **To:**, **Cc:** or **Bcc:**.

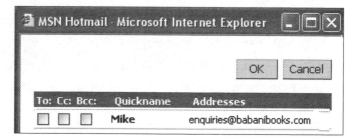

MSN Hotmail - Microsoft Internet Explorer

OK   Cancel

To: Cc: Bcc: Quickname   Addresses

☐ ☐ ☐   Mike   enquiries@babanibooks.com

- Text in messages can be enhanced with the help of a range of different formatting and editing tools.

E-mail Attachments

An attachment is a file which is "clipped" onto an e-mail and sent with it. The attachment could be a report done on a word processor, a spreadsheet, a drawing or a photograph. This would enable you, for example, to send a family photograph to friends or relatives in Australia or America.

If you do a lot of work with photographs, Windows XP has a **Filmstrip** option in the **View** menu allowing you to scroll through your photograph collections on CD or hard disc.

If you are planning to send a lot of photographs or very large files as attachments to e-mails, it is worth considering a Broadband connection as discussed earlier. Photographs can take a long time to send and receive by e-mail, using an ordinary modem. Broadband would enable you to send photographs to friends and relatives around the world in a fraction of the time taken using a conventional modem.

If you do send photographs by a conventional modem, they should have been saved as **.jpg** (or **.jpeg**) files. This is a special compact file format used for photographs. You might also *compress* photographic files using a program such as Paint Shop Pro. This program can also be used to save photographs as files in the **.jpg** format. For example, a photograph might have been originally saved as a **.bmp** file, the standard Windows graphics file format. The **.bmp** file would be loaded into a program like Paint Shop Pro. Then it is re-saved in the normal manner but with the file name extension **.jpg** added, such as **harvest.jpg**, for example.

Sending an Attachment

The general method for sending an attachment is the same whatever e-mail program you are using. The new e-mail message is addressed in the **To:** bar and the text typed in the usual way. Then you select the **Attach:** menu option or click the **Attach** icon to bring up the **Insert Attachment** window shown below. This allows you to browse through the folders on your hard disc to find the file you wish to attach to your e-mail.

After clicking the **Attach:** button shown on the previous screenshot, the name of the attached file appears in the **Attach:** bar in the e-mail window as shown below.

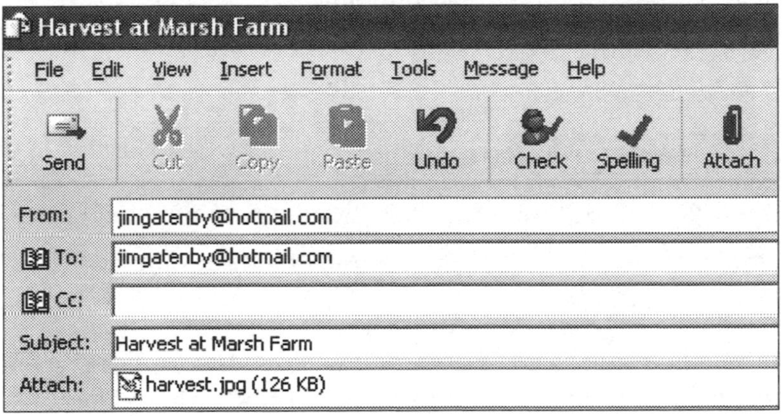

As shown above, you can test your system by sending a message, with an attachment, to your own e-mail address.

Receiving an E-mail Attachment

After you click **Send**, the e-mail and its attachment will travel to the **Inbox** of your intended contact. The presence of the attachment in the **Inbox** is indicated by a paperclip symbol next to the entry for the e-mail as shown below.

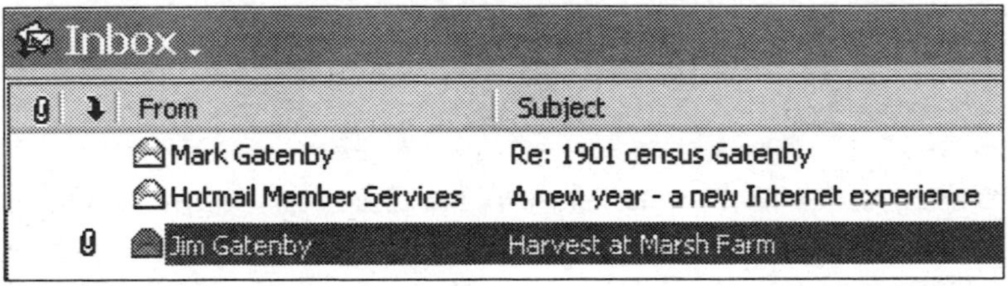

When the e-mail is opened by double-clicking its **Inbox** entry as shown in the above screenshot, the name of the attachment appears in the **Attach:** bar as shown in first two screenshots on the next page.

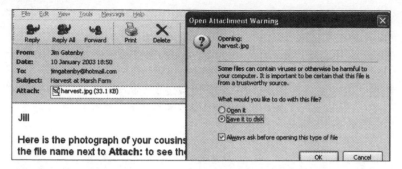

First you need to double-click the name of the attachment,

harvest.jpg, as shown above and on the right. Then, in Outlook Express, the **Open**

Subject:	Harvest at Marsh Farm
Attach:	harvest.jpg (33.1 KB)

Attachment Warning shown below asks you to either open the attached file or save it to a folder on your hard disc.

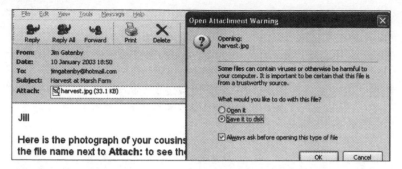

All e-mail attachments should be checked before opening them, using an anti-virus program like Norton AntiVirus or Dr. Solomon's Anti-Virus Toolkit. If you are using MSN Hotmail, incoming and outgoing attachments are checked automatically using McAfee VirusScan.

The Windows Media Player

Introduction

Windows XP and Windows Me include the popular feature, Windows Media Player. Amongst other things, this allows you to create a library of your favourite music and play and edit video clips on your computer. So, for example, a relative could e-mail a video clip of their children which you could view on your own computer. You can choose from a long list of designs, known as *skins* for the appearance of your virtual media player, such as the Windows Classic design shown below.

The Windows Media Player is far more versatile than a conventional music centre or video player. The following is a list of some of the things you can do with the Windows Media Player:

- Play your favourite music in the background while working away at the computer on a task such as word processing, etc.

- Copy music from CDs to your hard disc, so that you no longer need to find and insert CDs.

- Organise and manage audio and video files by creating your own playlists in the **Media Library**.

- Obtain details of audio albums and video clips such as artist, track name and genre from the Internet.

- "Burn" your own audio CDs by copying music from your hard disc to the CD.

- Download or "stream" (play directly) audio and video clips from the Internet.

- Use the **Radio Tuner** to find and listen to radio stations of all types on the Internet across the world.

- Choose from a range of **Visualisations** - animated patterns which move in time with the music. An ample number of visualizations are supplied and you can download even more from the Internet.

- Change the styling of your on-screen media player using the **Skin Chooser**.

- Watch video clips and edit them in Windows Movie Maker. (Part of Windows XP rather than the Media Player but included as it is a multi-media feature).

Starting to Use the Media Player

The media player is part of Windows XP and Windows Me and can be launched from **start, All Programs** and **Windows Media Player**. (If you do not have Windows XP or Windows Me, the media player is available separately).

The media player can also be started by placing an audio CD in the drive, then selecting **Play Audio CD** as shown below in the Audio CD window which appears.

Audio CD (D:)

Windows can perform the same action each time you insert a disk or connect a device with this kind of file:

Music CD

What do you want Windows to do?

Play Audio CD
using Windows Media Player

Open folder to view files
using Windows Explorer

Take no action

The media player opens in its own window occupying the whole screen, as shown below. Down the left-hand side are seven buttons used to select the main components of the media player. The buttons are **Now Playing, Media Guide, Copy from CD, Media Library, Radio Tuner, Copy to CD or Device** and **Skin Chooser.**

The Windows Media Player has the usual **Play, Stop, Forward** and **Reverse** buttons, etc. The centre of the **Now Playing** window shown above is occupied by a constantly changing artistic display, which moves in time with the music. This display is known as a **Visualization** and a large number of alternative designs are available. You can change the visualization from the currently selected **Battery: brightsphere** by scrolling through the available list using the two arrows at the bottom left of the **Now Playing** window as shown on the left.

To use the media player for background music while freeing the screen for other tasks, click the minimize button (shown right) on the top right of the window. The media player will continue as an icon and name (shown right) on the Windows Taskbar at the bottom of the screen. Click the icon to restore the media player to its full size.

Skin Mode

The media player can be switched between the **Full Mode** (shown previously) and the **Skin Mode** shown below. This is done by selecting **Skin Mode** from the **View** menu across the top of the media player window in **Full Mode** or by clicking the icon (shown right) on the lower right of the media player. In the screenshot below the Windows Media Player is shown in **Skin Mode** against a background of the Windows Desktop.

Copying Music from CDs to Your Computer

It's very convenient to make copies of your favourite CD tracks onto your hard disc. The means that the music you enjoy is always available while you are working at the computer. You don't have to search around for CDs and keep swapping them in the drive. You can also copy just a selection of your favourite tracks and it's possible to organize these in personalized playlists.

To begin the copy process, place the required CD in the drive and select the **Copy from CD** button. By default, all of the tracks are ticked, but you can exclude tracks by clicking to remove the tick. Click the **Copy Music** button to start the copying process. The **Copy Music** button changes to **Stop Copy** as shown below.

The Media Library

After you have copied the CD, its details are displayed in the **Media Library**, accessed via its own button on the left of the media player. The **Media Library** lists all of your audio and video files and allows you to compile your own playlists, using the **New playlist** and **Add to playlist** buttons.

When you place a new CD in the drive, the media player starts up and plays the tracks. If you click the **Copy from CD** button, the window is mapped out to show all of the details of the CD. However, in the case of a new CD, many of the details may be missing such as the artist's name and the musical genre. If your computer can be connected to the

Internet, you may be able to obtain this information using the **Get Names** button shown on the left.

Once the album and track information have been found on the Internet it's automatically entered into the **Media Library** - there's no need to enter any information manually.

You can organize your favourite music into playlists after selecting the **New Playlist** button.

Playing Music from CD or Hard Disc

To play music from a CD, simply insert the CD in the drive and the media player will start up automatically with the **Now Playing** feature selected. To play music which has been copied to your hard disc, start the media player and open up the **Media Library**. Select the required playlist or album and click the **Play** button to start the music.

The **Now Playing** feature gives access to a range of additional features and controls. The centre of the window displays the currently selected visualization. You can cycle through the visualizations using the arrows, shown, in this example, next to **Ambience: Random**.

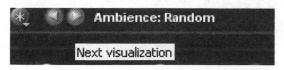

The Media Guide

Clicking this button connects you to the Internet and onto a Web page hosted by **WindowsMedia.com**. On this page are links to topical films, music and video. These can be downloaded to your computer or broadcast directly for immediate listening or viewing. In this process, known as "streaming", the multimedia files are not recorded on your hard disc. If you connect to the Internet via a conventional modem, the performance of streamed video is limited. *Broadband connections*, such as ADSL and cable modems, operating at least ten times faster than the traditional modem, are much more suitable for streaming video.

Copying Music from Your Hard Disc to a CD

Windows XP includes its own CD burning software, described earlier in this book for the copying of data files to CD. CD-R media can only be used for one recording session, while music copied to CD-RW may not be compatible with certain types of CD player.

To copy music from your hard disc to a CD, open the **Media Library** and highlight the album you wish to copy. Then click **Copy to CD or Device** on the media player.

The Radio Tuner

When you select the **Radio Tuner** button, you will be automatically connected to the Internet, assuming you have a modem and Internet connection set up and working correctly. Your media player will display a set of Internet radio stations from around the world. In addition you can search for a particular station using a range of search criteria such as keywords, the **Genre** (Oldies, Classical, Rock, etc.) the **Frequency** and the **Country**.

Windows Movie Maker

This component of Windows XP and Me allows you to view and edit videos. The program is launched from **start**, **All Programs**, **Accessories** and **Windows Movie Maker**. You can view a sample video provided in Windows XP by selecting **File, Import..., My Documents** and **My Videos** then selecting **Windows Movie Maker Sample File.wmv**.

Select **Open** and a series of clips are created as shown above in the middle panel. The video is divided into clips for ease of editing. A clip can be edited by cutting or trimming and a voice-over can be added.

The *timeline* along the bottom simulates a piece of film. Clips can be dragged and dropped onto the timeline to make a film in a particular sequence. Then the complete film can be played by selecting **Play Entire Storyboard /Timeline** from the **Play** menu. Video clips can be sent to friends and relatives as e-mail **attachments**.

Index